HE
HIT
ME FIRST

Louise Bates Ames

HE HIT ME FIRST

When Brothers and Sisters Fight

with
Carol Chase Haber
and
The Gesell Institute of
Human Development

Dembner Books   New York

Dembner Books
Published by Red Dembner Enterprises Corp., 1841 Broadway,
New York, N. Y. 10023
Distributed by W. W. Norton & Company, Inc., 500 Fifth Avenue,
New York, N. Y. 10110

Copyright © 1982 by Louise Bates Ames and Carol Chase Haber.
All rights reserved.
Printed in the United States of America.

Library of Congress Cataloging in Publication Data

Ames, Louise Bates.
    He hit me first.

    Bibliography: p.
    Includes index.
    1. Sibling rivalry.   2. Child psychology.   3. Parent-
ing.   I. Haber, Carol Chase.   II. Title.
HQ772.A473   649'.143   82-1565
ISBN 0-934878-18-8   AACR2
ISBN 0-934878-34-X (pbk.)

To Tom, Tommy, Doug, Greg, and Karen Haber

Grateful acknowledgment is made to the following for the use of quoted material:

From *Positive Parenthood,* copyright © 1977 by Paul S. Graubard, used with permission of the publisher, The Bobbs-Merrill Company, Inc.

Delacorte Press from *Raising Siblings* by Andrew G. and Carole E. Calladine. Copyright © 1979 by Andrew and Carole Calladine. Reprinted with permission.

Delacorte Press/Seymour Lawrence from *On Becoming a Family* by Dr. T. Berry Brazelton, copyright © 1981 by T. Berry Brazelton. Reprinted with permission.

Excerpts from *I Should Have Seen It Coming When the Rabbit Died* by Teresa Bloomingdale, copyright © 1977 by Teresa Bloomingdale. Reprinted by permission of Doubleday & Company.

Reprinted by permission of Farrar, Straus & Giroux, Inc. Excerpt from *Dale Loves Sophie to Death* by Robb Foreman Dew. Copyright © 1981 by Robb Foreman Dew. This material first appeared in *The New Yorker.*

Harper & Row from *How to Grandparent* by Fitzhugh Dodson, copyright © 1981 by Fitzhugh Dodson. Reprinted with permission.

Holt, Rinehart and Winston, Inc., from *The Siblings* by Brian Sutton-Smith and B. G. Rosenberg. Copyright © 1970 by Holt, Rinehart and Winston, Inc. Reprinted by permission of Holt, Rinehart and Winston.

Little, Brown and Company from *Growing With Your Children* by Herbert Kohl. Copyright © 1979 by Herbert Kohl. Reprinted with permission.

Meadowbrook Press from *Best Practical Parenting Tips* by Vicki Lansky. Copyright © 1980 by Vicki Lansky. Reprinted with permission.

Nash from *How to Father* by Fitzhugh Dodson. Copyright © 1974 by Fitzhugh Dodson. Reprinted with permission.

Reprinted with permission of P. E. I. Books from *Raising Cain and Abel Too* by Dr. John McDermott. Copyright © by John McDermott.

Sovereign Books from *Allergies and the Hyperactive Child* by Doris J. Rapp, copyright © 1979 by Doris J. Rapp. Reprinted with permission.

Westview Press from *Violence and the Family* ed. by Maurice R. Green, copyright © 1980. Reprinted with permission.

Contents

7

Preface

This book was motivated by a question asked by a member of a Los Angeles lecture audience. It was five-thirty in the afternoon of an intense day-long program in Parenting Preschoolers. A panel of eight lecturers was on the stage for a final hour of questions and answers.

Some of the questions asked were answerable even in the brief time available. But one, "How can I keep my children from fighting with each other?" seemed inappropriate.

Nobody can tell you, in five minutes or in fifty-five, how to keep your children from fighting. (As one realistic mother once phrased it, "Keeping my children from fighting would be like keeping them from breathing.")

At any rate, it was at that moment that this book was born. Nobody we know of can tell you how to keep your children from fighting. But in the space of a book it should be possible to give suggestions that could make family living, in some families at least, a little more comfortable, a little more friendly, a little less contentious than it ordinarily is.

One way that this can be done is for parents to lower their expectations—to be a little more realistic than many are as to the

amount of harmony they should expect. A great deal of quarreling, even of violence, does take place in perfectly normal households. Parents who can face and accept that fact can approach
the whole business of parenting with useful realism.

Another help in parenting is to know a little about what child
behavior is like at different age levels, and what will—and will
not—motivate young people.

It can also help if you are able to face the fact that children
differ. Some are by nature relatively friendly and uncontentious.
Others, right from earliest childhood, are programmed by their
genes to fight every inch of the way.

We appreciate, of course, that this whole subject of brother
and sister relationships is by no means virgin territory. Nor do
we hold a corner on suggestions as to how to keep your children
from fighting. Recognizing this, we have cited the work of others
and have quoted some of the best advice they have had to offer.
The numbers in parentheses, throughout the text, are keyed to
these references, which are given in full on pages 179 through
181. The book that we have found most helpful in understanding
the relations between brothers and sisters is Andrew and Carole
Calladine's *Raising Siblings* (11). We recommend that book as
a supplement to our own.

Admittedly *What to Do, and How to Do It* books for parents
abound. Specific advice about every aspect of child care is nowadays readily available. But the Gesell approach has been somewhat different from many others. We prefer to think of *you* as
the specialist on the needs of *your* child.

In thinking about child behavior we, like others, tend to focus
on three things: the child's individuality, his age, and the effect
of the environment on this particular child at this particular age.

In most of our books we have described primarily the first two
of these variables—what personality differences and the different
ages are like. We then have preferred to let you come to your
own conclusions as to what you—a major part of the environment—should do about the whole thing.

Parent demand, nowadays, seems to be for something more than mere information. Parents seek rather specific suggestions as to what they should *do*, even what they should *say*, under various circumstances.

Thus the present book is a combination of two rather different approaches. We do, as always, give information as to what behavior *in general* is like, at different ages and for different kinds of children. But we also include much rather specific advice as to things that parents can do to make life at home with their children more harmonious, more comfortable.

However, it is important to remember that, in spite of any advice that we or anyone else may give, nobody knows your own children better than you. You are the expert on your own boy or girl. Only you can decide whether things you read are helpful for you and your family.

Good luck!

Chapter One
Who? Why? When?

"Why do you children fight all the time?" . . . "Why can't you get along better?" . . . "Why can't you be nice to each other the way other children are?" . . . "Why do you have to spoil things for all of us with your constant bickering?"

Good questions, all of them, but largely unanswerable.

Sometimes we tend to make things seem worse than they are by what we *tell ourselves* about them. Actually most children *don't* fight all the time. (Most sleep at night.) And while their fighting is admittedly irritating, aggravating, annoying, and tiresome, does it or need it actually spoil your family living? Agreed it makes things unpleasant for *you,* but do *they* really suffer?

So instead of interrogating your children, how about asking *yourselves* some questions: Is it all really so bad? Do your children fight "all the time" or just much of the time? Do the children in other families really get along all that much better?

You may find that it helps to group the questions you ask yourselves under the following headings: Who? Why? and When? Let's take "Why" first, because it's the big one and has so many answers.

Why?

This tends to be a highly individual matter, but possibly the main reason children fight is because they enjoy it and it gives them something interesting to do. There are few things that bring more sheer pleasure to the ordinary boy or girl than a good fight with a brother or sister. In fact it may be fair to say that, more often than not, the harder the child yells, the better time he is having. Not only is it fun to fight, but there is always the delicious possibility that parents may blame the other child and that this will get him* in trouble. In fact this may be one of the most gratifying payoffs of any quarreling—the delightful hope that one may get a sibling into difficulty.

Even the smaller or weaker of two children, the one who always gets the worst of it, often enjoys fighting and squabbling. Once he has been rescued from his bigger brother or sister (and his life saved, to hear him tell it) a few minutes later he is right back in the danger zone, doing exactly the thing he knows will start up the battle all over again.

Thus, to begin with, children fight because they like to and because it fills the time. Busy, happily occupied boys and girls are less likely to fight than those with time on their hands and nothing to do. However, every set of children undoubtedly has its own particular reasons for quarreling. Chances are that with a little detective work you can figure it out for your own family.

A major reason why children fight is that nearly all are competing desperately for their parents' approval, love, and attention. Nearly all of us like to come first and be the best, and this desire is tremendously strong in the young. Many children would like

*Unless some specific child is being discussed, "he" should always be read as "he or she." It seems to us less cumbersome to use the generic "he." Also for the most part, so far as sibling relationships are concerned, sex differences are less important in affecting behavior than are those of age, individuality, or circumstance.

to be the only child and to do away entirely with hated rivals for their parents' approval. Most are jealous of their siblings because—whether it is actually the case or not—they feel that their parents love the others best.

Another strong reason for squabbling among the very young is that they are not yet old enough to share. Their possessions are to them a part of their very selves. (Did you ever note the way an eighteen monther may not even permit you to put your hand on the arm of his chair? The chair is to him part of himself, his turf, and he doesn't want anybody to touch it. How much harder to share a toy for which he may actually have some need!)

Another reason why siblings treat each other badly is that they are often mad at the world, and it is much safer to take things out on a sibling than on a parent or teacher. If a boy or girl is feeling out of sorts, unhappy, or ugly, as many do, what better victim than a younger or weaker sibling?

As we grow older, it is sometimes easier to live and let live, but the very young tend to be highly demanding about the way other people should behave. It is usually not too fruitful to try to change or to complain about the way one's parents behave—easier and more effective to complain about a sibling.

Then there is the ever pressing and never solved question of fairness. Since it is virtually impossible to keep everything totally fair in any household, many occasions inevitably arise in which one sibling will be given more privilege or possession than another. Rage rises. Complaining and quarreling result.

Some younger siblings fight to show those older that they cannot be bossed around. Older siblings fight to prove that they *can* control the young.

But it is not only that some brothers and sisters quite naturally "take it out on" each other when things go wrong in their lives. Some boys and girls, one must admit, are just naturally somewhat mean, cruel, and irritable. They like to see others made uncomfortable. What better victim than a nearby sib? In that case you have a special situation which requires very special treatment.

Since there is seldom enough of everything—time, love, money, privilege—to go around, in a family there are just more things to fight about than in other kinds of situations. If, for instance, the whole family decides to go skiing—as parents may desire or the majority may wish—that child who prefers to do something else will lose out. Surely grounds for complaint!

One of the more usual causes of quarreling between siblings is that one or the other is in the way—sitting in your chair, usurping the telephone, breaking your toy, wearing your clothes, looking at your goldfish. Opportunities for irritation and annoyance are endless, even in a well-run, orderly, and basically comfortable household.

Having to take care of a younger sibling, having him tag along when you want to be free to do your own grown-up thing, is a source of vast annoyance to many in their teens.

And—there's more—as Paul Ackerman and Murray Kappelman point out (1), one of the biggest reasons any child behaves badly with siblings is to get attention. We are all aware that, so long as things are going along peacefully, most of us will not pay too much attention to the young. Many children find from practical experience that the way to attract parental attention is to do something highly unacceptable. What easier or more available target than a sibling?

Certainly nobody would claim that all fighting between siblings is benign. But some psychiatrists, like Dr. Richard A. Gardner in his lively and useful book *Understanding Children* (21), go so far as to suggest that "a fight a day keeps the psychiatrist away." Gardner feels that fighting between brothers and sisters is a manifestation of irrepressible, healthy forces within the child. In fact, he believes that any child who does not express at least some degree of sibling rivalry may be an inhibited child who has been defeated by those around him in his struggle for self-expression.

Our list of Whys need not be longer. Most of you can add to it almost indefinitely. We might summarize by saying that, like the person who climbed the mountain, many children fight with their siblings because they are there.

Who and When?

The answers to the question "Who fights" can be brief, and you may find that they are often intertwined. Certain combinations of children at certain ages and in certain situations are guaranteed to be combustive. Not all quarrels are predictable but a surprising number are.

Clearly, if you have only two children in your family, they are the ones who are going to be doing the fighting. But if you have three or four, you may find that it tends to be only certain combinations that guarantee discord.

"When?" If you stop to evaluate the situation objectively, you may find that the most, and the worst, fighting usually occurs at certain times of day. The most usual time is just before dinner when children are hungry, cross, and tired.

In fact, some pediatricians go so far as to suggest feeding your children all or part of their meal half an hour or an hour before the working parent comes home and the main meal of the day takes place. There is some evidence that when a child is hungry, the part of his brain that controls socially acceptable behavior may not be properly nourished or properly functioning. If this happens, there is nothing to inhibit violent or unacceptable behavior. If you don't want to go so far as to serve your children's dinner ahead of time, perhaps you could serve them a snack.

In addition to just-before-dinner, there may be other periods when fighting commonly occurs. Zeroing in on these times and situations is a good first step toward prevention—if that is your ambitious aim.

Or of course it may be duration that makes the difficulty, and not just the specific time of day. If our children are getting along nicely for the moment, many of us, overestimating their endurance, let things go on too long. You may find that while your children keep the peace for half an hour at a time, a whole hour may be too much.

Though we generally do recommend what some refer to as "benign neglect," the subject of children's fighting needs a little homework on the parents' part. Once you know the Why, Who, and When of your youngsters' major difficulties, you can perhaps prevent many fights from occurring.

Edith Neisser (37) rather long ago discussed, very helpfully, what she called the structure of a squabble or "the anatomy of bickering":

> Every quarrel, every argument, even every downright fight between children in the same family may be thought of as having three layers:
>
> 1. First the immediate cause of the trouble,
> 2. The struggle for status,
> 3. The underlying core of resentment accumulated from years of rivalry for possession of the parent.

Neisser also gives this rather good advice: "If quarrels repeatedly follow the same pattern or occur at the same time, appreciate that *the structure of a squabble may be the clue to its cause.*"

It may take quite a bit of detective work to figure things out. And the very best detective work won't put an end to all quarreling. But it most certainly can reduce it.

In short, you may get much farther in providing family harmony if, instead of asking, "How do I *stop* them from fighting?" you ask yourself the more constructive question "What can I do about their fighting?"

A Few Basic Suggestions

Here are a few basic rules and suggestions, which we shall repeat and elaborate on as this book proceeds:

1. Keep in mind that most siblings fight a good deal of the time and that for the most part they enjoy it.

2. If it really bothers you, do your best to stay in a part of the house where you can't see or hear them.

3. If one or the other is actually getting physically harmed, separate them. In fact, you'd be wise to make a rule that no sib is allowed to harm another physically. (You may not be able to enforce this rule all the time, but it is a good one to make.)

4. Do not allow yourself to be habitually dragged into things, as judge and jury.

5. If it seems to you that your children fight with each other "all the time," try looking at the other side of the coin. Try focusing on the amount of time during which they play peacefully or even enjoy each other and do nice things to help, support, or comfort each other.

6. Whenever you can, try to take a long-range view of things. Remember that sibling relationships in most families tend to get better as time (much time) goes on.

7. In the meantime, keep in mind that when you are called on to step in, as you often will be, an overcharged situation may sometimes be defused by relatively simple techniques.

8. Remember that the more their fighting bugs you, the more attention it calls to themselves, the more they will fight.

9. Instead of asking yourself, "How can I keep my kids from fighting?" put your question positively: "How can I help my children get on better than they do now?"

10. You can handle sibling rivalry most effectively if you can bring yourself to think of it as a normal part of development and not as a total threat to family happiness.

11. Perhaps a parent's best and surest recipe for peace of mind is to expect considerable conflict, appreciate its normalness, do what you can to manage it. But keep in mind that fighting and squabbling are for many children a way of life. They enjoy it. Even the very young child tends to have a very strong sense of

self-preservation. Most could avoid a major part of their fighting *if they really wanted to*.

Things Do Get Better

Encouragingly, sibling relationships *do* get better with age. We can practically guarantee this. Of course there are the occasional adult brother and sister who "haven't spoken for years." But such a situation is comparatively rare, and even they are inclined to be quiet about it and no longer bug one another.

In Chapter 12 we discuss this anticipated improvement step by step, age by age, in considerable detail. Here we'll just note some of the more customary stages of sibling adjustment (or nonadjustment).

Dr. John F. McDermott (33) puts it as well as anybody when he identifies four customary stages through which most brothers and sisters pass in their relationships as they move on toward adulthood. In the very first of these stages, which he calls "Might Equals Right," each child wants all of everything. "Mine" is the most-used word.

We have often commented that the typical two-and-a-half year old wants complete possession of any object he is playing with, has played with, or might play with. While this madness is at its height, there is really very little that one can do about it. We once observed two-and-a-half year old Tommy in his playroom—his cart filled with all the toys it could hold, his arms and legs outflung protecting as many other objects as he could pile on the floor beside his cart. Whenever his younger brother Doug attempted to touch anything either within Tommy's physical range or even in other parts of the room, Tommy would cry out angrily, "Mine!" (He of course couldn't play with *any* of these things because he was so busy protecting them.)

When Grandmother finally asked Mom, "Doesn't anything in

this room belong to Douggie?'' Mom replied calmly, ''Tommy doesn't think so.''

But once this passion for total possession has started to pass its peak, mothers can begin to use typical nursery-school techniques to induce a bit of sharing or taking turns. Lectures tend to fall on deaf ears. But one can suggest, ''What else could Douggie use?'' or ''Pretty soon it will be Douggie's turn'' or—often most effective of all—''But Douggie *needs* it.''

If one is fortunate, this kind of prompting does eventually catch on, and by the time many boys and girls have reached age three or a little after, they may spontaneously use some of these phrases on friends who are reluctant to part with desirable objects. Sharing will always be difficult for some but probably never as difficult as when the child is in the two-and-a-half year old stage when he seems to *need* to possess everything in sight.

The stage that immediately follows ''Might Equals Right'' is called by McDermott ''You Scratch My Back and I'll Scratch Yours.'' During this stage, a flimsy truce may at times be arrived at.

Doing unto others as you would have them do unto you is practiced, to some extent, not because it's moral but because that way you're more likely to get what you want out of life. It's the favor-exchange principle at work: Each builds a bank account of favors with others through negotiation. If someone does a favor for you, you have an obligation. It may not get at the root cause of sibling rivalry, but it can begin to reduce the intensity of fighting.

And then, moving along, we come to the Law and Order Stage—''It's Not Fair, You're Cheating.'' At this stage many can make fairly firm rules with one another, as for instance the rule that each will not go into the other's room without permission. They may even, realizing that violation of the rule will be inevitable, spell out penalties for infraction.

And finally—and this stage arrives late with many, in high school or even in college—we come to the ''As Brothers and

Sisters Go, You're Not So Bad.'' As McDermott warns, "If brothers and sisters do begin to show genuine respect for each other, don't expect them to admit it openly. Don't rub their noses in it. The best you can expect is for them to admit grudgingly that their brother or sister really isn't so bad after all, compared to others they know.''

So inevitably, it is a long road to harmony, consistent or lasting, but it is a road that does have a turning.

Chapter Two
Dos, Don'ts, and Discipline

Don'ts

Since it tends to be easier to tell people what *not* to do than what *to* do, we shall, perhaps a bit presumptuously, list some of the Don'ts that we and others have found useful in helping children in a family to get on with each other:

To begin with, *don't* act as a referee. At least don't do it any more than you will inevitably have to. What every child longs to hear is your verdict that "You were right and your brother [sister] was wrong" . . . "She was wrong to go into your room" . . . "He was the one who started it. No wonder you hit him back." Try to avoid such definitive verdicts.

There will inevitably be times (often many of them in a single day) when you will be called upon to settle some dispute. Sometimes you can get out of it by saying, "You settle it yourselves." Or when some ill-doing on the part of a sibling is reported, you can say, "Well, what are you going to do about it?" (Admittedly, on occasion you will be confronted with a situation which you cannot weasel out of with all the good techniques in the world.)

Don't intervene in "normal" bickering. If somebody is getting murdered, you will usually know it by the volume of the cries. (Or by the loudness of the silence.) The more you can manage to stay out of things, the more ingenious and self-reliant your children will become in settling their own squabbles.

Don't reward tattling by encouraging it. And even if one of your children does seem to you most often to be the cause or center of quarrels, *don't,* if you can help it, give him the poor self-image of feeling that "everything" is "always" his fault.

Don't insist on getting to the bottom of things in the hope of finding out who was "really" to blame. There are rare instances when it is absolutely necessary for you to know how the whole thing started and who did what to whom and when. But much of the time the whole story will be so convoluted, and often only slightly related to the truth of the matter, and each of two or three combatants will be so dedicated to proving that he or she was the innocent victim, that the most skilled efforts cannot get to the true facts.

Most fighting between siblings has long and tangled roots. The one who seems on the surface to have "started it" may actually be the victim of a clever conniver. *He* messed up her paper dolls, it may be true. But *she* swiped his bubble gum (slightly used, perhaps, but he was saving it) first. And before that he *bothered* her when she and her friends were playing house. (Et cetera, et cetera, et cetera.)

Also, any formal inquisition achieves just the result you were trying to avoid. It attracts your attention, takes up your time, and encourages your children in the hope of achieving victory over an (often) hated rival.

Thus *don't* allow your children to draw you into a pattern of spending a vast amount of time and energy discussing and trying to straighten out their disagreements. Keep such sessions as few and brief as possible. Don't be a patsy.

In other words, *don't* let the children's fighting and your efforts to control it take up any more of your time than you can possibly help. Don't let it become the major issue in your household. Part of any child's motivation in fighting is to get your attention. Don't let it pay off.

Don't set yourself up by allowing repetition of situations which you know aren't going to work. For instance, if your six-year-old, like most, absolutely cannot stand to lose a competitive game, don't permit him to play such games with, let's say, a demanding eight-year-old. Or not often, anyway. Fighting, blaming, and name calling is almost certain to result.

Don't bemoan loudly, often, and in the children's presence that they "fight all the time" and you just cannot stand it or do anything about it. Most children are ready and eager to live up to such advance billing, especially when it is negative. Instead of moaning, keep your anxieties to yourself and try to do something about the quarreling.

Any child in any family is likely to feel that his parents "always" favor the other(s). This can't be helped. *Don't* add fuel to the fire by allowing yourself to favor one or the other conspicuously, even though your heart may urge you to do so. You very likely *will* have a favorite, but try not to make this grossly obvious. And *don't* encourage hostile competition by forcing the children to compete for your attention.

In fact, *don't,* at least in their presence, compare your children to each other. Don't hold one up as an example to the other(s): "Why can't you mind what I say the way your sister does?" Or even worse and even more unanswerable, don't say to a child, "Why can't you be a satisfaction to us the way your brother is?" *Don't* compare them with relatives or children in other families who, according to you, behave perfectly.

Don't go on and on about some misbehavior which is now safely in the past.

Don't push sex differences, as by telling your daughter she can't do this or that because she is "only" a girl.

Don't allow your children to play you against your spouse. In all likelihood one of you will be a little more lenient, one a little more strict, than the other. This is natural and not necessarily harmful. But do your best not to let the children capitalize on it or use it to gain favors. Do your best to back each other up. If you can't manage this, perhaps one could have charge of certain activities or areas of behavior and one of others.

If you are the homebound parent, *don't* take all the blame for the way the children behave. Though many children do behave a little better for their father than their mother (they are usually more afraid of him), if he feels that you are doing a "lousy" job with them and their bickering, arrange that he be the person in charge at least for a while.

Don't set unrealistic goals with regard to the degree of family harmony that you expect. Start where you actually are and then try, little by little, to improve matters. Don't start out with some inaccessible goal and then berate your children and criticize yourself because that goal is not reached. Thus do not expect or require total sharing, utter fairness, lovely peace.

Don't allow yourself to overidentify. For instance, try to avoid overidentifying with your poor darling daughter who is always being picked on by her mean big brother. If anything can cloud a clear evaluation of a present situation, it can be an overidentification with your own past.

Dos

And now for the Dos. To begin with, *do* keep in mind that most children fight. A lot.

Although we've warned you not to try to get to the bottom of every quarrel, *do* try to find out why your children fight. (The reasons may be so deep-seated—basic hatred, desperate jealousy—that they will be hard to deal with. But the reason might be a small or specific thing that you could do something about.)

Try making *need* rather than *fairness* the basis for decisions. Things never do come out fairly, and even if they did, the children wouldn't think so. So get whatever it is for the child who needs it, not for every child in the family.

Do keep in mind that whatever you do—how cleverly you arrange your children's time and play situations, how superbly you set things up—many times they are going to fight anyway. If you avoid one kind of material that normally makes trouble, they will find another to quarrel about. Chances are that if you were down to one set of blocks, with plenty for both, they would quarrel about these.

However, *do* avoid situations that, by their very nature, will cause difficulty. If two boys under four have each a box of pennies, each is bound to believe that the other has some of *his* pennies.

Do separate your children more than you may be doing. Break up bad combinations so far as you reasonably can.

Do use "rules." Many children, especially preschoolers, tend to be absolutely snowed if you tell them that something is "the rule." To make this work, make rules simple and specific. Avoid big, general rules such as "You must be good to your sister." Instead state specifically: "You are not to hit your sister."

Do what you can to make each child feel special. Spend as much time alone with each as you possibly can.   *Do* help children protect their most prized possessions. You can't keep siblings from *looking* at them, but at least do all you can to keep a child's very best things from being destroyed.

Do try to help your child find varied outlets for emotions, so that fighting with siblings will not be the primary pleasure.

Do help (older) children not to let others get a rise out of them. Teach them that if they ignore misbehavior, it may not be repeated. Teach them that age-old bit of doggerel, "Sticks and stones can break my bones, but words will never hurt me."

Unless children are vastly ill matched, do all you can to encourage them to work out their own solutions to problems.

If you know that a certain kind of situation always turns out badly, but that situation cannot be avoided entirely, try to step in before the lid blows off.

Try using Behavior Modification techniques. That is, reward behavior that you wish to have repeated. So far as you can stand it, ignore the bad.

Do all you can to reduce tattling by making it unrewarding. Unless the behavior reported sounds definitely serious, say, "Oh, is that so?" and show by your indifference that tattling isn't going to get anybody very far. On the other hand, if the report demands some action on your part, say something like, "Thank you for telling me that Bobby broke the glass. I'll pick up the pieces."

Do try to help your children figure out their role in the family. Help them not to try for a dominance for which age and personality make them unsuited.

Do on occasion try role playing or role reversal. Thus let a younger child play the role of an older child and vice versa. This can on occasion be both entertaining and effective.

Do when necessary take advantage of that extremely useful device—Time Out. The child is sent to his room and told that he cannot come out till the timer rings. For many children, the timer seems to have almost magic power. Many even quite violent children will wait passively till the timer rings before they dare to emerge. However, for some, it works best if, instead of setting the timer, you merely tell them they can come out when they are "ready" to be good.

Be aware that, as Herbert Kohl (30) puts it, many fights tend to dissipate by themselves—one of the children leaves the room, a friend comes over, something funny or unexpected happens, and they forget what they are fighting about. However, Kohl also says:

> There are times when things seem to get serious and the children don't know how to get out of the situation. The tone of a serious fight is unmistakable. If I'm around and hear that sound, I simply move in and separate the children, either by telling them to go to different parts of the house, telling a joke to distract them, offering

them a snack if they seem hungry, or by taking one of them away
by force as a last resort.

When the quarreling and fighting in the household seem to
have reached extremes, here's a trick that some find to be extremely helpful: Keep a diary, list, or chart—anything that will
objectify the situation. This device can give you a realistic picture
of just how bad (or good) things really are.

A chart of the timing of friendly harmonious play and actual
quarreling and fighting might show that on the average your
children can play together nicely for, let's say, half an hour or
even more before fighting breaks out. Or it might demonstrate
that some certain times of day or special kinds of activity or some
certain combinations of children may be at the root of most
difficulties.

Knowing what the pattern actually is can sometimes help you
know what to avoid. Often it can also cheer you up by showing
that things in your household are much better than you had feared.

McDermott (33) supports this suggestion with the following
comment:

> Just as you go to your pediatrician for the children's physical
> checkup, you yourself can make a checkup for patterns of sibling
> relationships. If you do this periodically, you will not only note
> changes and be able to respond to them, but you will identify pat-
> terns, problem areas, and potentially dangerous situations so you
> can then arrange to minimize them or at least be present to super-
> vise them.
>
> Count the number of fights. Note what they're about: i.e., pa-
> rental attention, possessions, physical space, games, whatever.
> Also note the times when things go well. In school-age children, if
> fighting occurs almost all of the time they're together and they
> seem unhappy more of the time than they are happy, this may sig-
> nal a problem that goes beyond "normal" sibling rivalry. Listen
> and watch at mealtimes to see the percentage of reasonably pleas-
> ant discussions versus arguments and disagreements.
>
> When one child complains to you about another, it often works

to ask the complainer what he intends to do about it. This approach sometimes encourages children to resolve their own conflicts. In fact, perhaps a more constructive and less abrupt method is, before any special conflict starts or any complaint is uttered, to encourage your children to study their siblings, to get to understand them, and to work out ways of handling them that may bring good results. One of our own ten-year-old friends reports the following success in this direction:

> Well, Jill, you may know, is the lazy and absent-minded type of character; so we don't really get along too well because Mother says I'm systematic. Every morning we have a system where we all three wash dishes. Right after we finish—it's past eight-thirty—because school starts at quarter of nine Mummy will drive us to school.
>
> Usually Bill and I do the dishes, and Jill sits there and reads. So one morning we thought up a good plan. She was saying, like she always does, "Bill, you didn't finish your cereal" . . . "Jenny, you didn't eat your bacon" . . . "Jenny, you didn't feed the dog." And if anybody says "I did," she kicks them.
>
> So this day, Bill washed real fast and I washed real fast, and I wiped off the shelf and the oven and everything. And then we went and got some flowers for our teachers, and got into our coats and ran off. And Jill was stuck there and she had to wipe the dishes and put them away all alone. And I have a feeling she felt sad that we weren't there, 'cause she couldn't tease us. So now I think she's got the idea. But I think we've got to keep it up for a few more days, because usually she doesn't respond to things very fast.

If children are very angry at each other, just telling them not to hit or hurt each other does little to defuse their anger. This may sound rather quirky, but some parents find it works well to suggest to two sibs who are fighting that each draw the ugliest picture possible of the other. This serves two purposes. It tells them that you understand they *are* angry at each other, and it gives them a chance to vent their anger in an acceptable manner.

Another trick that some parents find helpful is, when two (rather young) children are angry at each other, to try seating them in chairs that face each other but are far enough apart that they do not touch. Make them sit in these chairs, staring at each other but not talking or touching. Chances are that within a few minutes the ridiculousness of the situation will hit them, and they will burst out laughing.

Another useful thing, if there seems to you an abnormal amount of quarreling in your household, is to check your children's health. An allergic or otherwise unhealthy child tends to be irritable and to get into much more trouble than one who feels well.

If things are really horrendous, do feel free to get outside help. Family therapy, as we shall comment later, has saved many a family's sanity. And for yourself, take some time off from your family each day—certainly each week. Anything looks better if you can get away from it, even briefly.

The Six S's of Harmonious Family Living

A sort of grand summary of things to do to help your children get along with each other has been called (49) the Six S's of Harmonious Family Living. They are separation, space, scheduling, something-else-to-do, supervision, and surprise.

Separation may be your best bet. Clearly, children can't fight with each other very effectively if they are not together. But nice as it would be if young ones could just be shoved outdoors together or older ones sent to the family room, where they would all get along peaceably, in some families this is *not* the case. So, if need be, by whatever hook or crook, keep them apart.

Or, if you can convince yourself that they really are not doing any harm (to objects or themselves), let them stay together and separate them from *you*. If you can't see or hear them fighting, it will bother you much less.

A quite different kind of separation, which many recommend, is separation by ages. Some psychologists feel that, if your children are at least three years apart in age, their tendency to fight with each other and their pleasure in fighting will be greatly diminished.

Space, clearly, helps. Even if your house is rather small and your family rather large, you can usually arrange it so that they are playing in different areas. And if you are fortunate enough that each of your children has his own room, remember that *a child's room should be sacred.* He should not have to let the others in, since in a child's opinion just having someone *look* at his pet salamander may upset the salamander.

If separate rooms are not practical, and often they are not, it can help to draw a line (real or imaginary) down the middle of the room. Or some, as they grow older, can be satisfied by being given a private drawer for their prize possessions, a drawer that nobody is allowed to invade.

(If it is not practical for each child to have a room of his own, certainly all is not lost. Some children if given a choice prefer to share with a sibling. They enjoy the company even if it may cause a certain amount of conflict.)

Scheduling, if carefully worked out, can supplement or even take the place of space. This is easiest when children are young, but even at the older ages you can often plan a daily routine so that two or three quarrelsome youngsters will not be together, unoccupied and unsupervised, for long periods of time.

Something Else to Do. If you are fortunate, your children will be good at keeping themselves busy, but if they aren't, it will be up to you to provide, or at least suggest, activities. In nursery school, we have often observed that, if left to themselves with nothing interesting to do, children tend to revert to sex play. Similarly, at home children with nothing else to do tend to quarrel.

Supervision. This applies most effectively at the younger ages. You may discover that certain preschoolers need either your constant or your occasional supervision, or at least your intervention to keep things on an even keel.

A Surprise for Mother. With some children if things are incessantly bad, one can sometimes arrange for the child to plan with some outside person that *as a surprise for Mother* (or Father) they will try to do better. This person might plan with them as to ways in which their relationships could improve.

Disciplining a Whole Family

Discipline of course means much more than punishing, though one's way of disciplining is often interpreted as one's way of punishing. Discipline in its broadest sense means the way you run your home or your life. It is the flow and flavor of a household. It is the way you set things up so that life will go smoothly, quite as much as the way you handle problems once they have occurred.

In some households discipline is rigid and strict and consists of firm rules and regulations. In others, as one easygoing father recently explained to us, there are few special rules—things just kind of flow, and everyone pitches in to help with the work and to make things comfortable. On the other hand, if you have a home in which, as one mother put it, "There is nothing but screaming and yelling and hitting all day long," your discipline may be extremely faulty.

Much has been written on the general subject of discipline. We especially recommend Fitzhugh Dodson's *How to Discipline with Love* (16). Other fine books include those by Saf Lerman (32), Kohl (30), and Paul S. Graubard (25). But the most comprehensive, specific, and useful suggestions for disciplining a whole family of children are those of the Calladines (11). We quote their basic rules:

1. Try to eliminate physical punishment in your household. It merely teaches that if you are bigger, you can hit.

2. If there is trouble, try setting the kitchen timer for a calming time when siblings must sit apart from each other. The timer successfully takes your nagging voice out of things. If the bickering continues after play is resumed, a stronger discipline tool will obviously have to be used.

3. Try taking away a relevant privilege from the children when house rules are abused. (Of course this means that you will have set up house rules to begin with.)

4. Remove any fought-over object for a realistic period of time.

5. Securely hold from behind any physically attacking sibling.

6. Give suitable work assignments to all angry siblings to channel their aggression and to get some constructive use from this powerful drive.

7. Learn to ignore and stay out of sibling power plays for parental attention.

8. If problems arise about turns, have the children pick a number from one to ten to see who is closest to a chosen number, and therefore gets the first turn.

9. If at all possible, stop a growing struggle before it snowballs completely out of control.

10. If quarreling is vigorous, isolate the children until they can indulge in good group play.

11. If fist fighting, biting or slugging is occurring, separate and isolate the children.

12. On the other hand, isolate yourself if you find that you are becoming irritable. Disciplining siblings works best when you are in control and can use a calm voice.

13. Praise and praise and praise, whenever you suitably can. Also be sure that you communicate with your children as fully and freely when things are going well as when they are going badly. Don't make them feel that they have to behave badly to get your full attention.

14. Change the activity that is causing a sibling dispute. Give them something better to do.

15. Role-play a sibling scene. Have the children change places to discover how the other sibling feels.

16. Try to teach your children the power of words to work out

agreements, compromises, contracts. Words can be the most powerful tool of all in teaching siblings how to get along—your words and *their* words.

Chapter Three
You Can't Always Win

The Wish to Be Loved Most

Underlying a great deal of the bickering, fighting, quarreling, disagreeing that goes on in the usual family is the ordinary child's abiding desire to be his parent's absolute favorite. Everyone wants to be loved best, liked most, totally preferred. A sixty-year-old woman of our acquaintance once had a dream in which her mother said, "Aggie, you are my favorite child. You are better than your brother."

Most of us never do hear those words, and it would be a rather impractical parent who would utter them. Any child, given this much encouragement, would immediately share it, in a taunting way, with siblings, and then the fat really would be in the fire.

How a parent handles this overwhelming need to be first, to be loved best, to be the chosen one, varies of course from family to family, but few manage to do a really superior job in solving the problem.

Certainly much hedging, much sparring, much double-talk is bound to be involved, and however tactfully a parent puts it, short of making an absolute flat statement of favoritism (which is what the child really wants), he is apt not to give satisfaction.

When children are very young, if by chance you have only one of each sex, it's relatively easy to say things to the effect that "You are my very favorite little boy" (or "girl" as the case may be). Even when they are older, this theme can often be emphasized satisfactorily.

Obviously if there is more than one girl or boy, this rather simplistic gambit won't work.

Since what the child wants to hear ("You are my very best one") cannot in all safety be said, your best course is probably this. Do everything within your power to make each of your children feel loved, cherished, appreciated, admired, important to you. This won't be what he or she seeks—to be the *very* best—but it can give enough feeling of personal satisfaction that, even though the supreme wish cannot be granted, it won't be quite so vital anymore.

And, to be useful, this time when you make the child feel loved, important, and admired cannot wait until he gets good grades in school, or wins the debating contest, or earns high honors in athletics. This time has to be right from the very beginning.

It isn't difficult to pay attention to a baby. For most people there are few magnets stronger than a tiny baby. It's hard to keep our hands off him. And if he is our own, his every achievement seems fascinating and noteworthy.

This extreme fascination wears off slightly as the baby becomes a preschooler. Most preschoolers are so extremely demanding of time and attention that we tend to tire of them long before they tire of us. Our advice is, go that extra step.

Your preschooler babbles on, or wants you to read to him, or to sit and watch his favorite television program, at a time when you haven't a moment to spare. Spare that moment anyway. (And for the child of any age, time alone with you can help. If you have half an hour to spare and three children, it is perhaps best to give each one ten minutes alone—rather than spend half an hour with all three together.)

So, admire your child's new abilities: He can ride his tricycle, she can pile her blocks, he can paddle around in the swimming pool. "Watch me, Mom" is a constant cry.

Help him enjoy the holidays. One mother we know reported cheerfully, "Halloween was a great success. It took only a day to make Billy an elephant costume; and the two smaller boys used the clown suits I made last year." It takes a lot of time, but we guarantee it's worth it.

Admittedly they take much, if not everything, for granted for many years. But surely the feeling is building that they are important to their Mother. More security, less need to fight.

But that need to be first and to be loved best *is* there. Dodson (15) comments realistically:

> It is important to understand the basic cause of sibling rivalry: Each child deep down wishes he could somehow get rid of his brothers and sisters and have 100% of his parents' love and attention. This is the reason for the almost constant bickering and fighting that goes on between brothers and sisters. *Once this basic cause of their rivalry is understood, you can see that sibling fighting can never be eliminated from a family; it can only be moderated.*

Playing Favorites

Let us say that in all wisdom you do avoid actually *saying* to any one of your children that he is your favorite. How do you actually *feel?*

Most parents tend to feel an extraordinary love and admiration for all of their children. It comes with the territory. But many of us do, admittedly, have a very special favorite. Almost beyond reason, some one child may seem to us just exactly right. Most of you have seen that very special smile that curves the lips of a mother when she looks at what seems to her that very perfect child.

This favorite child is by no means always the handsomest, the smartest, the kindest, the most thoughtful. Many forces that the parent himself may not recognize go into that very special response to one certain child. The important thing is not to feel guilty about such favoritism. We often cannot control our feelings. But we can control our actions.

Thus while it can be quite natural and fair to *feel* a preference for one child or the other, the wise parent will do everything possible not to *demonstrate* it too openly. Your feelings may be fairly obvious to the rest of the family, but it is your responsibility to do everything within your power not to play favorites.

Try not to be like the mother who, in the days of long skirts, spoke sharply to what she thought was her three-year-old daughter: "Annette, get away from my skirts." Then looking down she saw her mistake and cooed in a kindly voice, "Oh, it's Bobby" (her one-year-old son). Annette remembered this incident long after she was a grown woman with children of her own.

Must Everything Always Be Fair?

How can you as parents keep things fair for all your children, a demand that they will make of you time and again? In fact this is one of the loudest and most frequent complaints in any family: "It isn't fair" . . . "He got the biggest piece" . . . "You *always* let him have more turns than me" . . . "It isn't fair that he gets to choose the programs" . . . "It isn't fair that he stays up later than I do" . . . "It isn't fair that she gets a bigger allowance" . . . "It isn't fair that she gets to have her friends stay over and I don't" . . . "I have to *find* something decent to wear. She goes to her closet and *chooses*" . . . "It's not my turn to do the dishes."

This demand for fairness extends not merely to opportunities and privileges. It includes material things as well. Whatever one child has of any nature whatever, the others want at the very least an equal share.

So how do you as parents manage to see to it that everything in your household is always scrupulously fair? The answer is that you don't. Any parent who allows himself to play the fairness game has had it, right from the start. As McDermott has pointed out correctly (33), "A family is not a democracy."

Everything between individuals cannot possibly be scrupulously even. There is no reason it should be. Life itself isn't fair, and things seldom come out entirely even. It is very important for any parent to make this absolutely clear to all his children from the start.

Nowadays there is a certain political pressure toward insisting that all persons are equal. Equal in the eyes of the law, perhaps, but certainly not equal as individuals. The sooner the children in a family appreciate this, the more comfortable for all concerned.

The Calladines (11) make the sensible suggestion that each child should be treated as an important individual, and that comparisons should be kept to a minimum:

> If you can look at treating your children as individuals as an adventure in discovering their me-ness, rather than their sameness, you will bank selfish sibling fires. Making things fair is a game that doesn't work in families. In fact, equality stinks.
>
> Life isn't fair. Why teach your children that it is? We have a much better option. There is a richness of differences, a richness of differing needs, a richness of differing dreams in our children.
>
> Children have a way of keeping close tabs in a family that plays the fairness game. They know when you're guilty. You know it, too. Instead of trying to be scrupulously "fair" about everything, try teaching your children that there is a difference between measured fairness for all and being fair to each child based on what is needed and is available to give. If in your family a child gets what he needs when he needs it, all of your children will be reassured of their specialness.

These, then, are two important things to keep in mind whenever questions of fairness come up. Think of each child as an individual, a very special person. And think of each one in terms of his own needs, not in terms of what you are doing for or giving to somebody else.

One special example is the matter of birthdays. In some families every child is given some little token when a sibling has a birthday, so they won't feel left out of things. Much better to come right out and face the fact that this is Billy's birthday, not somebody else's, and that Billy is the special person on this day and the person who gets the gifts and the special attention.

Another example is that of a family of preschoolers in which the rule prevailed that Daddy could take only one person when he went on an errand, never two. Though now and then some little voice would pipe up, "Could you take two today, Daddy?" whenever the answer was "No," as it usually was, all accepted very calmly the fact that not everybody got to go everywhere every time.

One reasonably safe rule is this. Even though you cannot and probably should not try to treat all your children just the same or to give all the same privileges or opportunities, try to avoid doing something for one that will work a definite hardship on the others. This doesn't mean to avoid anything that they *think* works a hardship on them. It means something that would cause actual, unnecessary deprivation, as for instance sending one child to a superexpensive college with the result that the others would be unable to go to college at all.

No attitude in the world will entirely prevent demands for fairness, tortured complaints that things are not being fair. But a calm, unimpassioned attitude on your part can most certainly reduce these complaints and these demands. Children are very quick to sense their parents' vulnerability or lack of vulnerability. Few continue for long with ways of behaving that are never rewarded, demands that are never met.

Getting Even

Getting even with him. How many hours of childhood are spent in getting even with brothers and sisters! It may not be very nice, but it certainly is very natural.

Some of our nicest children not only spend their time this way, but shamelessly admit to doing it. Ten-year-old Jarvis tells us, "My sister's so funny. She's so afraid she's going to get poisoned. If she is eating one of the best things and you say it might be poison, she won't eat it. Like I might say, 'These cherries taste funny,' and she would think they were poison and wouldn't eat them for a million dollars. That's one of my best ways of getting back at her."

Or nine-year-old Nicky, when asked why he interrupted his sister's piano practice by tootling on his horn, tells his mother, "Because she's so bossy. She always tries to raise me and make me do everything better, and this is the best way I know of to get even with her."

Eleven-year-old Teena explains, "Well, what I do with my brother and sister, I try to get every bit of evidence I can against them so that when they do anything mean to me, I can get even with them and end up by being the right person." That is, the situation may not even have arisen yet, but she plans to be ready if it does.

If you have more than one child in the family, we suspect that getting even is a phenomenon with which you are quite familiar. It is, of course, an immature way of dealing with a situation in which another person offends or harms us. Gradually as your child matures you may find that you are able to help him find more effective ways of dealing with distressing situations. But it will take a certain degree of maturity on his part and considerable skill on yours. And even if and when you are able to control his *actions,* you cannot necessarily control his *thoughts.*

Mommie's Home—Everybody Cry

There are other situations in which it is hard for a mother to come out ahead. One of these is aptly titled, "Mommy's home—everybody cry."

It is one of the curses of motherhood that children who all afternoon have behaved "like angels," according to baby-sitter, aunt, or grandmother, suddenly all burst into tears, complaints, and squabbling the minute Mom comes through the door.

Most children are at their best, but also at their worst, with their mothers. Many children, especially infants, demonstrate their new abilities (their first word, first step) to their mothers—and often won't repeat the performance, when requested, for others.

On the other hand, children of all ages *take things out* on their mothers, behave with them much worse than they would dream of with others. Those modern fathers who bring up their children alone inevitably attract the behavior normally reserved for the mothering, or care-taking, person, and tend to have the same kinds of experiences. Their children love them best, but undoubtedly behave the worst when in their company.

"I'll Break Both Your Legs"

Conscientious parents often worry grievously over the terrible things that they say to their children in moments of stress. In retrospect, many fear they may have done permanent harm to the children's psyches.

We ourselves have been reminded that we are not exempt. We have been known to say things as extreme as "You little creep, I'll break both your legs if you kick him again," or even more drastic, "I'll kill you if you don't stop doing that."

Not very friendly, we'll admit, but perfectly natural. There comes that moment when even the most saintly would snap.

Fortunately, so far as we know, the damage done is not permanent. In fact it may not even be temporary.

Children have a reasonably keen ability to evaluate their parents. Most know that you are not going to kill them or even break both their legs. They take your threats for what they are worth—an expression of deep but momentary frustration.

A situation that tends to bring out the very worst behavior on the part of children, and some of the most violent reactions on the part of parents, is the long family ride in a car. A good example of the violence that such a trip is likely to induce, as well as of the relative calm with which children tend to accept rather wild threats on the part of their parents, is given by Robb Forman Dew in *Dale Loves Sophie to Death* (14).

Martin and Dinah were driving their three children to their summer home. The children were edgy and cross and this year even the youngest, Sarah, was old enough to join the melee.

"Toby's looking out my window, Mama! He's looking out *my* window!"

"Toby's sitting in the middle. What can he do?"

"I didn't look out his window when I was sitting in the middle."

"Oh, Mama, Toby's . . ."

And then Dinah half turned in her seat and stared at them with furious hatred, and all three children were immediately filled with remorse.

"Well damn it, Martin, stop the car," she said in deadly, measured calm. "Stop this damned car! There's only one answer to this!" Her voice was so ominously low that the children looked away from her in nervous discomfort. And Dinah herself, with the blood beating in her ears in irrational fury, was not paying attention, either. In her rage she chose not to see the effect of her anger. "We will just put out Toby's eyes! We will just, God damn it, put his eyes out!"

She turned to stare at them more directly and she gripped the back of the seat with one tense hand. At last, her voice rising, she said, "Will *that* make you happy, Sarah? Then, I swear to God, he will never look out of your window again! That should do it. . . ."

Martin, of course, had not stopped the car and, in fact, was driving on placidly enough. "Look! We're getting close," he said to the children. "See what landmarks you can find."

The children gladly followed his suggestion. . . . These children knew that their mother loved them, and they knew that their father loved them. They even had an accurate impression of their parents as they were in relation to each other—united. By and large the Howell family was one in which, in the long run, each member possessed mercy and compassion toward each other member. Even Sarah, at age four, had already perceived enough to know that her mother would die—really would die—before she would put out Toby's eyes. She quite rightly absorbed her mother's fury as a rebuke to herself, and she continued to wipe at her tears furtively, and so she missed the first major landmark.

Following the same theme, though a little more mildly, we have the true story of Priscilla, aged six. She was being very naughty indeed—so naughty, in fact, that her normally gentle mother said to her, "Priscilla, you know I not only don't love you, I don't even like you." Priscilla replied very calmly, "Mummy, you love me, and you know you love me." She was right. Her mother did love her, except perhaps in moments of vast exasperation.

So, our position is that though it is best not to make wild and violent threats to your children, all is not lost if now and then you do. Blowing off steam should be, and usually can be (by both parent and child), differentiated from the kind of angry, ugly, threats a parent may make with every intent of carrying them out. Nor are we talking about child abusers. They in all likelihood act more than they talk, or act as they talk. We are speaking of normally calm, patient, responsible parents who, even as you and I, sometimes get totally fed up.

So don't worry if now and then you do utter threats that, as you look back on them, seem like pretty terrible things to have said. We forgive you, and feel quite certain that your child will do so as well.

Chapter Four

Come On Out
and Fight

This problem has been discussed so many times that it is by now at least a cracked if not broken record. And yet, for each family—if it is going to have more than one child—the questions are always the same: How do we tell the old baby that there is going to be a new baby? How do we prepare him for its arrival? What arrangements should we make for him while Mother is in the hospital? What do we do after we bring the baby home to prevent or at least reduce jealousy? What do we do if he *is* jealous?

The answers to all these questions seem to us to involve more common sense than anything especially "psychological." They also depend a good deal on the temperament of the particular child involved.

A child's basic personality or temperament combines with the way life has treated him to determine the way he will feel about a new baby (and potential rival). Some are like the little girl who on being shown her new brother, John, requested, "Mo jon, mo jon, fo fo" (which translates into "I want to see more John. Put him on the floor where I can see him").

Others are not so friendly. One little boy is reported to have pressed his nose against his mother's protuberant abdomen with the threat, "Come on out and fight." Or, the seven-year-old daughter of one of our colleagues, who had insisted on having a baby brother or sister, two months before the baby was to be born asked her mother, "Why are you having this baby?" Mother replied truthfully, "Because you said you wanted it." The little girl countered with "Whatever made me say a thing like that?"

So, the joy and enthusiasm with which you announce the coming event will be tempered by your own knowledge of your child and your evaluation of what his or her response is likely to be.

Preparing a Child for the Arrival of the New Baby

One can hardly spring a baby on an entirely unprepared sibling. But telling him about the prospective arrival of a new baby, like telling him about sex, should not be too difficult. You know the facts. The trick is to give this information calmly, coolly, clearly, in an unembarrassed manner, and not to tell too much too soon.

The secret of success may lie not so much in what you do as in what you do not do. It is extremely important not to give this information too soon. The very young child has a different time sense from the adult. A month to him can seem forever, so if you tell him about the new baby, say, six months in advance, he may get very tired indeed of the long wait.

We have the story of a mother who planned to go on a business trip with her husband. With some trepidation she told her three-year-old daughter that Mom and Dad were going on a visit and would be gone for three weeks. Later in the day the little girl asked her mother, "Mom, did you say three weeks or three years?"

At any rate, unless the child asks questions, best delay the announcement till the last month or so.

Chances are that he will ask. Though we once knew a ten-year-old boy who seemed quite oblivious to the fact that his mother was very shortly to have a baby, many children, even quite young ones, do notice that Mother is changing in form and, often, behavior, and they want to know why. When the child inquires is an ideal time to give him needed information. But if he does not ask, you will have to bring up the topic yourself.

Do your best not to get the child's hopes up too much. Tell about the baby in simple, clear, uncomplicated terms. And by all means avoid giving the impression that the new arrival will be a barrel of fun. Be quite honest about a new baby's smallness and lack of mobility, and within reason do mention the fact that the baby will cry a lot and will need quite a lot of care and protection. Also, of course, do not promise specifically that the baby will be a boy (or a girl) unless amniocentesis has revealed this to you.

Try not to tell too much. The entire detail of how the baby is conceived need not be shared with the very young. Fortunately almost any public library or bookstore has many fine books that help the expectant mother tell her child the main and necessary facts about a new baby. One of the best is *Betsy's Baby Brother* by Gunilla Wolde (Random House). This book explains very clearly how helpless and demanding a new baby can be. It discusses the fact that a child might on occasion feel jealous and even wish the family could give the baby away. And then it shows that a little girl can help her mother in caring for a new baby and that will make her feel better.

Another very dear book about new babies is titled *When the New Baby Comes, I'm Moving out* by Martha Alexander (Dial). Oliver is *not* happy about the prospect that his mother is going to have a new baby. But his mother helps him to see that there are many advantages in being a big brother.

Another pair of books (you will see that we are very strong on the use of books in a crisis) that should prove very helpful are *Making Babies: An Open Family Book for Parents and Children Together* and *That New Baby* by Sara Bonnett Stein (Walker &

Company). These charming picture books cover almost any question that might come up, either before or after the baby is born.

Reading such books to your child not only gives the information he needs, but also allows him a good opportunity to ventilate his feelings.

In addition to all the talk that may or may not be involved, many mothers find that some preschoolers enjoy short shopping trips for the purpose of buying things for the baby. Quite obviously such trips must be planned with the stamina and staying power of a youngster in mind. The trip should be short, undemanding, fun. And most certainly there should be some purchase or purchases for the child himself. We do not believe that everything has to be fair or to come out even. But under the circumstance that a new baby (a rather large unknown) is descending on the family, it is only humane to go out of one's way to make the soon-to-be-displaced young person feel that he is still of major importance.

Other arrangements around the house will very likely be going on in the weeks or months preceding the birth of the baby. It is very important here that the child not be given the impression that his crib, high chair, powdering table, or any of his paraphernalia are going to be ruthlessly taken from him and handed over to the new arrival.

We prefer that a child not be moved from his crib to his big bed much before the age of four. If your child is around four years of age, it would be possible first to buy his new bed and then to make plans with him for the new baby to sleep in his old crib (if that is to be the case). Arrangements about changing or sharing rooms should be made with equal care. Whatever the new plan is to be, it is essential to do everything within your power to make the older child *not* feel that he is being displaced.

Probably your very best clue, in conversation, book reading, shopping, or planning for the new baby is your own child's interest. Go along with it. If the whole matter appears to be of special interest, devote considerable time to it. On the other hand, if he doesn't seem to care, he may just not be ready for this kind of concern. So don't dwell on it.

What Arrangements for the Older Child While Mother Is in the Hospital?

In those not-so-long-ago days when new mothers stayed in the hospital for a good two weeks, what to do about the older children in the family used to pose a serious problem. Some parents felt that there was less disruption if the children could remain at home with some trusted and familiar care-taker. Others believed that going to Grandma's (if Grandma was available and if the child was accustomed to visiting with her) might be the most comfortable solution.

Nowadays hospital visits are so short, and new-baby leave for fathers so much more easily obtainable than in the past, that in many families it now seems to work out best if the child remains in his own home, with Father or some familiar relative or housekeeper in charge.

Some very advanced thinkers believe that not only Father but a sibling should be permitted in the delivery room. But this seems a most questionable gambit. In fact with the hospital visit currently so short, some feel that any hospital visiting by the child might best be omitted, and the introduction to the new baby planned for in the familiarity of his own home. Others find that a brief hospital visit to see the new baby and to check out that Mother is OK is useful and fun for all concerned.

How About Jealousy?

Much everyday, sensible advice has been written about what to do when you bring the new baby home. The old wisdom is still good. Most young children are rightfully apprehensive when this new member of the family first makes its appearance. Common sense tells you not to make too big a deal of this event. Downplay the baby. He won't care. Play up the fact that here you are at home and very happy (as you undoubtedly will be) to see your big boy or girl.

Then in the first days and weeks, busy and tired as you surely will be, do whatever you reasonably can to make your child feel that life is not too different from what it was before. Spend as much time with him as you reasonably can. If there is outside help, when possible have the helper take care of the baby while you concern yourself with the older child.

Some people advise not having the older child see you when you breast-feed the baby, because this event may arouse some rather peculiar feelings in him. But most authorities agree that the more natural you make life seem, the better for all concerned. Admittedly some children, when they first see the baby nursing, misbehave to take your time and attention from this process. They get into trouble, break things, cry and whine, have a bowel movement, anything that (they feel) needs immediate attention.

However, by the time you have a second child, chances are that the breast-feeding will not seem all that big a deal to you, and you will be able to combine it with a reasonable amount of attention to your older one. The majority of children do accept this function with relative calm. As one two-and-a-half-year-old explained to his grandmother as Mother nursed the baby, "He's just havin' his lunch."

One of the biggest helps we have observed is for Mother and Father to refer to the newcomer as New Brother or New Sister, an unthreatening and accurate way to describe the newborn. Calling the infant Your Baby, as some do, seems a masterpiece of overstatement. New Brother or New Sister, on the other hand, makes it clear in a matter-of-fact way that this is just a new and accepted family member.

But however careful you are, some jealousy will raise its ugly head. It comes in different forms and at different times. Some children, right from the beginning, will not accept a new arrival: "Why don't you take him back to the hospital?" . . . "Why don't you give her away?" . . . "I don't like her." Others seem friendly and even loving early on, only to take a turn for the worse when the baby becomes mobile and therefore more of a nuisance and an attention getter.

Sometimes jealousy takes the form of too-hard hugs, too-devouring kisses. Or it comes right out in the form of hitting or straight-arm slugging. We have known a preschooler to approach her baby brother with a large, sharp knife and obvious intent to harm. That is, some jealousy disguises itself but can still be hurtful, whereas in other cases there is absolutely no question about the older child's intention—he wants to do the baby in.

Jealousy symptoms or no, it is never wise to leave an untended, unprotected infant with an older sibling under the age of six or seven. This may sound extreme, but it's best to err on the side of overcaution. It's fine to make such family rules as "We do not hurt anybody, and that includes the baby." But if you aren't there on the scene, you won't be available to enforce the rule when enforcement may be sorely needed.

A baby doll for brother or sister, a doll that he or she can dress and undress, powder, change, put to bed, and pretend to feed, often helps. Once the baby is mobile, it also helps to prepare a fairly safe place for the older child's "things," a baby-proof place. Your time and attention and anything you can possibly do to make a child feel that he is important to you can help even more.

Many consider a so-called geographical cure, that is, removing a child from a possible trouble spot, to be the part of weakness. Not so in the present instance. Sending your older child to nursery school, if a good one is available in your community, can be one of your very best cures for jealousy. And, of course, not only nursery school. Keeping a child happily occupied, providing him with as rich and full a life as possible, reduces his need to obtain emotional satisfaction by feeling and expressing jealousy, especially of a new baby.

Your older child's age and level of emotional security will naturally influence his reaction to the baby. A child over three or under eighteen months usually reacts more favorably to the coming baby than one who is in between these ages. We know of a two-and-a-half year old who, at the time of his mother's pregnancy, was going through a usual but very strong stage of reliving his babyhood. In addition to other babyish ways of behaving he insisted on being called not by his own name but by the appelation ''Baby.'' When he was finally told that there was to be a new baby in the family, he insisted, ''No baby. I Baby.''

At any rate, the way your young child accepts the news, and eventually the presence, of a new baby depends in part on your own handling of the situation, but it also depends, at least in part, on the older child's age and temperament.

In most cases no matter how well adjusted your child or how good your own techniques, some jealousy will be experienced. Vicki Lansky (31) gives the following specific suggestions for diluting what most of us consider quite normal and reasonable jealousy of a new baby.

> Express your own occasional annoyance with the baby's demands to your older child, but not so often that he or she gets the idea that the new sibling is a permanent nuisance. Express your joy, too.
>
> Put a stool next to the baby's dressing table so that your older child can watch changing and dressing routine.
>
> Let the child help as much as possible with ''our baby,'' holding, singing or talking to the baby and running errands around the house for you. Show your appreciation for the help.
>
> Set the baby's crib mattress at the lowest point so that an older child won't try to pick him or her up.
>
> ''Stall'' visitors who come to see the baby so that the older child can be the center of attention for a few minutes. Then let the child help you show the baby off.

Give the older child new privileges: a later bedtime, increased spending money or allowance, special things to do with a parent.

Get out the older child's baby pictures, especially those that show you giving him or her the same kinds of attention you now give the baby.

Have the baby bring the older child a gift from the hospital. Keep a few small surprise gifts on hand to give your older child when visitors bring gifts to the baby.

Take the baby to nursery school and let the older child show off his or her sibling at "show and tell" time.

Teach the older child that if he or she smiles often at the baby, the infant will soon return the smile. And show the child how to touch, love, and cuddle the baby.

And now here is a somewhat new angle on a well-worn theme. It is generally believed that when a married couple produces a new baby (assuming that the child was wanted), this baby is assimilated into the family without much difficulty. Some women, admittedly, find that motherhood takes a bit of getting used to. Likewise some men feel a bit displaced in their wife's affection by the newcomer. But for most it seems to be a rather matter-of-fact affair.

However, the experience of many parents suggests that a new baby can provide a very complex emotional problem even for a well-adjusted couple. The many facets of this problem, and helpful ways to deal with them, are discussed in Wolfson and DeLuca's *Couples With Children* (51).

Dr. T. Berry Brazelton, an innovative Boston physician, not only points out that becoming a family is a complex business, but comments on the effect that a parent's emotional attitude toward the new baby may have on an older child. His sympathetic and informative book *On Becoming a Family* (9) develops this theme. A father or mother, by his or her own actions, may actually exacerbate a preschooler's jealousy of a baby sibling. Brazelton points out that many perhaps overattached mothers actually feel, when they become pregnant with a second baby, that they are deserting the older child, in some way failing and depriving him of love.

He quotes one pregnant mother who, with tears in her eyes, blurted out in front of her preschooler, "But how can I leave Alice?" He believes that many mothers fear they cannot provide enough nurturing to go around. Many, he believes, do not themselves wish to dilute the intensity of their relationship with their older child.

Though we ourselves are a little cautious about telling a child "too soon" that there is to be a new baby in the family, Brazelton reports that many preschoolers who are unusually attuned to their mothers actually notice changes in her very early in her pregnancy. He feels that, if this is the case, a child should be told quite far in advance about the coming event.

> Given the chance to turn to their fathers or to their grandparents or to siblings, most children will begin to work out the coming separation. When the baby comes, the older child will be ready to share. [But] if his mother is upset by the impending separation, she may easily overprotect or hover over the older child so that he has less chance to find other resources.

Certainly some mothers hesitate and wonder as to when they should tell the child about the coming baby long after the child himself may be fully aware that something very big, different, and strange is happening to his mother. But Brazelton agrees with us that one can overdo preparation. It is a secret that should be shared, but it should not be talked to death.

Chapter Five

Does Position in the Family Influence Behavior?

Does a person's position within his family actually influence his behavior, and especially his behavior in relation to brothers and sisters? Some authorities believe that being the oldest, middle, or youngest individual in a family has no more influence on behavior than being born in some certain month. Others, fully reputable scientists, feel quite strongly that rank order within a family has a very definite bearing on behavior.

Among those best known for their interest in so-called rank order and life role are Walter Toman (48) and Lucille Forer (20). The following characterizations represent a composite of their work. Some consider such descriptions "mere" stereotypes. Admittedly many individuals will differ sharply from these descriptions of first-, second-, and third-born children. But it is important to keep in mind that stereotypes—even though they represent a certain simplification—contain much more than a grain of truth. They are developed from what people in real life have actually observed.

So here goes for what some expect, in a family of three, of the first-, second-, and third-born child.

First-, Second-, and Third-Born Children

It is generally accepted that *first-born children* are achievement oriented and often highly successful in their achievements—in fact are likely to become eminent later on. Even as children they may be capable, strong-willed, effective. They tend to have a high sense of responsibility, are likely to use words like "should" and "ought," and to want to conform and do things right. They tend to be conscientious in their studies. In fact their standards for themselves and others are often extremely high. When they are in the company of others, they like to be leaders. Relationships with parents are close and successful. First-borns often relate to their parents by developing strong drives of achievement.

We at Gesell have felt that first-borns, especially first-born males, tend to be hard to raise, though not everyone reports similar findings. Their many positive characteristics, however, make them rewarding later on.

First-borns, perhaps in part because of their usually good relationships with parents and their position of seniority in relation to siblings, often turn out to be secure, self-confident, and comfortable in and successful in positions of leadership.

Second or middle children are considered less highly driven toward accomplishment than their older siblings, more spontaneous and easygoing, more tactful, more adaptable, more relaxed, more patient, more emotionally stable, better able to balance opposing forces. They are less likely than the first-born to attain eminent status. A middle child has to learn ways of competing, but *indirect* ways, so he may become rather tricky or even sneaky. He may become a con-man or may merely learn diplomacy.

Second or later children give us, on the one hand, the paradox of greater autonomy and flexibility and, on the other, more consistent coping with siblings. They copy but they may also disassociate themselves and protest.

A second-born may feel that there are no unusual demands on him and that he *can* expect help from others. He may expect an older sibling to look out for him. He may be much less competitive than an older sibling, less driven to succeed.

The youngest child may feel somewhat inadequate and inferior, more passive and submissive, more accepting of domination, more babyish, less driven toward accomplishment and excellence, more quiet and withdrawn than those older. He may, even more than a middle child, develop indirect ways of getting what he wants. If he cannot get his own way, he may either give in or run to adults for support. He is by no means above either screaming or tattling. If he never gets his own way, he may become passive and withdraw from others when there is tension and threat in the environment.

However, in general, we do find that third children, especially when they are the youngest in the family, tend to be of a certain sweet and gentle disposition. Many seem to feel very secure in the feeling that there will always be somebody older to look out for them. This perhaps diminishes anxiety and strain.

Why Do First-Born Children Behave Differently from Those Who Are Born Later?

If we assume, as some do, that first-born children in a family behave differently from those born later, we are still faced with the question *why?*

Some maintain that the reason that first, second, and third (or other) children in a family behave differently from each other is because of the way they are treated by their parents and others.

Thus the argument goes, first children tend in later life to accomplish more than later-born children because their parents expect more of them. This being the parents' first experience with parenting, their expectations may be unrealistically high, their demands unduly severe. And the child tries to live up to these expectations and demands. Also, since he is for a time the only one the parents have to work on, they may place an undue amount of pressure on their first. And even after others are born, this first child is expected to set a good example, to take responsibility for the others.

Parents seem to expect less from a second child, to be less tense and demanding about his accomplishments or lack of accomplishments. By the time a third is born, many are quite relaxed about the whole thing. But they do tend to require the older child to be good to the youngest one. Thus their protectiveness (sometimes their overprotectiveness) leads the youngest to expect that other people will look out for him.

Irving Harris (27) suggests that the first-born's lifelong and special access to parents gives him a certain self-righteousness. Under attack he reacts with a stiffening of personal identity, whereas the later-born is more prepared to shift ground and to change one identity for another. The first-born is more consistent and rigid about his principles; the second-born is more pragmatic and deceptive.

All of this kind of thinking represents an environmental point of view—that children behave as they do because of the way somebody has treated them. An opposing view, and one that we find extremely intriguing, is that birth order may have some effect on the individual's development even before he is born. Some believe that for each pregnancy the intrauterine condition of the mother may be different. Not only that, but that each pregnancy of the mother may change these intrauterine conditions for subsequent children.

(We know this is true in the case of the negative Rh factor, in which a negative Rh baby, born to a positive Rh mother, influences her body in such a way that a second child may be in danger.)

Brian Sutton-Smith (47) has noted:

Birth conditions may be affected by the birth order of the child coming into the world. The duration of labor has been reported as much as fifty percent higher for first-born children, and the point has been made that they may therefore be subject to a higher degree of cerebral compression. Forceps are often necessary at the birth of first children, and such deliveries tend to be more hazardous than easier later births.

While there is not as yet any solid evidence on the matter, it appears as if the birth experience of being first-born rather than later-born may possibly introduce physical variations that have later psychological effects. The suggestion has been made, for example, that the first child gives off antigens, substances to which the mother reacts by creating antibodies, which in turn create a minor shock for the second-born, increasing his activity level. Whether or not the causal chain is as indicated here, in several studies second-borns have been shown to be more active babies.

These qualifications bear the warning that if first-born are physiologically distinctive, it is not impossible that many of the phenomena that are attributed to parental behavior may actually be, at least in part, stimulated by the offspring themselves. What has been attributed to parental shaping behavior may be a description only of one part of a complex synchrony between infant and mother, each being both active or reactive in different ways over a period of time.

So What Should We Expect as These Differences Relate to Sibling Relationships?

If we assume that these brief portraits of first, middle, and third children are anywhere near accurate (regardless of how they come about) and that they pertain in a general way to many or most children, what then would we expect all of this to mean in children's relationships with one another?

To begin with, even if these are fair portraits, any attempt to predict intersibling behavior from them must be a vast oversimplification. (For one thing many families have only one or two children or more than three.)

Sex differences must be counted in. Forer (20) gives examples of the many dissimilarities one might expect in even two-child families among the girl-girl family, the boy-boy family, the girl-boy family, and the boy-girl family. And this is with just two. Sutton-Smith (47) gives even more possible kinds of combinations by considering both age and sex, as discussed in Chapter 8 and shown in Tables 2 and 3, on pages 172 through 175.

A further variable, of course, is the basic inborn individuality of each child involved. For example, a gentle middle child sandwiched between strong, vigorous first and third would normally behave in a quite different way from one in a reverse situation—a second child vigorous and competitive by nature, born between older and younger siblings both very gentle in character.

For the time being, however, let us discuss what might be expected of supposedly typical firsts, seconds, and thirds in their relationship to each other.

First Child. This individual tends to be extremely bossy and domineering with his younger siblings. Very conscientious himself, he has strong feelings about what is right and wrong and about the way younger sibs should behave. He may have higher standards for them than their parents do. He doesn't like to see them get away with anything, especially things that he was not allowed to do at their age.

Being older and usually larger and more knowledgeable than they gives him a great advantage in his efforts to dominate those younger ones. Since he knows that he is likely to be blamed if left in charge of younger sibs and they misbehave, he may develop rather skillful techniques aimed at getting them to follow his lead.

Often when things are going well, the oldest sibling will make great efforts to entertain and protect those younger, and may actually do quite a lot to support and look after them.

(Though he is secure in being older and more capable, it must be remembered that the oldest child in any family is probably the one most deprived by the arrival of a brother or sister. He alone is the one who for a time has been an only child. All others have shared, to some extent, from the beginning.)

Second or Middle Child. It is generally believed that middle children tend to be more relaxed in their relations to siblings than do their older brother or sister. As a rule they do not expect always to get their own way—at least not by direct competition or head-on conflict. With siblings as with others, they learn to achieve what they want by indirect means. Thus a middle child learns to use whatever position is of value at the moment—that of being bigger and stronger than the little ones, or of being weaker than the older ones—to his advantage.

A second child faces from the very beginning the fact that not only are his parents larger and more powerful than he, but also his older sibling, who can to some extent command him, too.

If of a very competitive nature, he may engage in a lifelong struggle to equal his older sibling in accomplishments and privileges. More often, he is seen to accept his second place and to achieve what he wants by indirect (and even sneaky) means. He may find that he can get what is to him a more satisfactory reaction from an older sib by harassment rather than by physical attack.

If things go well between the two of them, a second child may look to his older sibling for support and protection. And although he quite normally will have the upper hand over any younger sib, he seldom takes on, even in this relationship, the full characteristics of the usually bossy and domineering older child.

Also since often he is less conscientious, it may not matter to him, as much as to his older sibling, that he or others do everything exactly right. Though he may fuss and fight and complain at times, in general he takes things more easily and is easier to get on with than the brother or sister who has just preceded him.

Third or Youngest Child. Dr. Frances L. Ilg of the Gesell Institute refers to this boy or girl as "that glorious third." This may be an apt description. It is not so much that this child is better endowed than those who came before. It is that he is, as a rule, easier to get on with.

With at least two older siblings, as well as parents, to order him around, as a rule he soon comes to accept the fact that he will get farther by going along with what is expected than by trying to compete.

Thus, if sharp, he soon learns that the best method of getting his own way is by being "nice," by going along with what others expect. He also may find that by being inconspicuous and rather quiet about his demands, he may be able to do what he wants a good deal of the time without having others notice.

Least of all does it appear that the average third child feels great deprivation or jealousy when and if a succeeing child is born to the family. For him, there has always been a crowd. He has never been the only one, and so he does not expect it.

Also, as many have pointed out, a group of three or more children in a family often develops its own subculture. They often seem to be a world to themselves. Thus many thirds derive great comfort and support from the presence of their older siblings, who are often good to them, protective of them, and pleased at and proud of their accomplishments. Older sibs often greatly enjoy "teaching" this younger member of the family.

Suggestions for Parents with Regard to First, Second, and Third Children

The following material has been adapted from Forer (20).

For Oldests. Try not to be too stern, demanding, and authoritative with your first child lest he later on adopt that role with others. Help him not to be too bossy and domineering himself.

Forgive his lapses from perfection. He will demand quite enough of himself.

Now and then baby him as you baby your youngest.

Help your oldest child to relax so that he will not overdo the "good, responsible child" role.

For Middles. Be sure that your middle child does not get lost in the shuffle. Occasionally single him out for special attention. But do not worry unduly because he is the middle child.

Try not to feel that "middleness" need be a special problem.

Be sure that he does not spend so much time adapting to the needs of others that he never gets a chance to be himself.

For Youngests. Don't let your older children treat the youngest as a toy.

Try to avoid letting them tease him, even though this is ostensibly done good naturedly.

Discourage his efforts to control by complaining and tattling.

Help him to learn to give, as well as to receive, with comfort.

Encourage him to behave in increasingly mature, responsible ways. Try at times to give him some of the responsibility you give your oldest.

Graubard (25) makes the interesting suggestion, which might work well with some, that if an older child feels jealous of a younger one, you could point out to him the privileges and responsibilities that age and competence bring. Then ask him if he would like to switch roles. If he agrees, exempt him from some of his regular duties, but insist that he go to bed at the younger child's bedtime and in other ways treat him as if he were younger. Any such "experiement" is likely to be very short-lived, as the older child rather quickly appreciates the disadvantages of being treated as though he were younger.

Siblings Make Each Other Different

Brothers and sisters obviously react to each other in their daily relationships. But in all likelihood they also have a more permanent effect on each other. Sutton-Smith (47) and others have suggested that siblings actually help determine at least some aspects of each others' personalities.

Personality is not infinitely flexible, but it does seem probable that any individual's manner of responding to the world, and even his feelings about self, can be strongly influenced by the way his siblings treat him. Whether the differences produced by siblings enter permanently into an individual's repertoire is not certain, but it seems quite possible that they do.

According to Sutton-Smith:

> Females are typically more affected by males than are males by females. Second-born are influenced by the characteristics of their older siblings. First-born and second-born siblings act like members of a dominance hierarchy, with the first-born showing the higher power tactics, and the second-born showing many forms of counterreaction, including aggression, against these power tactics.
>
> Each sibling is affected by the sex of the other siblings, and these effects are more obvious in the case of the younger siblings. It is the second-born who most faithfully reproduce in their own behavior the responses which have been modeled for them (and perhaps demanded of them) by their older siblings. Older siblings exercise more power over the younger siblings than vice versa.

Make Your Own Observations

Generalizations about the way first, second, and third children might be expected to react to each other are of course at best merely hypotheses. There will be many exceptions to any such rules. Observe for yourself whether or not your own children fit our proffered descriptions of firsts, seconds, and thirds. Note whether they do or do not interact with each other and influence each other in the ways we have proposed.

As we shall point out in the next chapter, a child's own basic inborn individuality may be so clearcut and dominant that it counteracts customary expectations as to the way a boy or girl in any family position might behave.

Thus a strongly mesomorphic individual, with a need to compete and to win, may be the most competitive of all, even though he may be a second or third child. On the other hand, a gently endomorphic individual, even though first born, may, with the endomorph's natural preference for peace and harmony, give in readily to other members of the family.

You as parents may find it of interest to check and to see whether it is your child's rank order in the family or his inborn individuality, or perhaps the way you treat him, that seems to influence behavior most.

Chapter Six
Every Child an Individual

"Infants are individuals" according to Dr. Arnold Gesell, who has written so much about them. So are human beings of other ages, from preschool to old age. And so are families.

The individuality (or personality) of the family is so complex that relatively few, except novelists, have written about it effectively. But the individuality of human beings, especially of children, has been studied and reported on at some length and with a certain degree of usefulness.

Understanding what each of your individual children is like does not certifiably predict how they will interact with each other. But it can provide clues and even hypotheses. So here goes!

Different Bodies Behave Differently

Children vary, not only in their reaction to one another but in their general response to life, all the way from the gentle, friendly, cooperative, and reasonable to the violent, critical, unreasonable, and even dangerous. For hundreds of years some students of human behavior have observed that human bodies come in different shapes as well as sizes and that people's behavior is related to the kind of body they have.

The most systematic investigation of this relationship we know of is that of Dr. William H. Sheldon and is known as Constitutional Psychology. This theory suggests that children—and grown people, too, for that matter—behave as they do to a very large extent because of the way their bodies are built. The popular generalizations—fat people tend to be friendly, muscular people tend to be athletic and active, thin people tend to be sensitive and shy—have long been held by many to be based on a certain amount of truth.

Yet the notion that we are not entirely free to behave as we wish or to make our children turn out as we wish is a hard one for many Americans to accept. As Margaret Mead once remarked, only if we find that we can *change* the body type will the study of physical differences as determining behavior become popular in American society.

There are two important beliefs underlying our own Gesell study of human behavior. One is that behavior changes in a patterned way with age. This notion has become well accepted by parents all over the world. People often write and tell *us* about it. But another idea—that behavior is a function of structure and that to a large extent an individual's behavior depends on the kind of body he has inherited—has been less popular and harder for many people to accept. Yet we believe it can help you to understand your own children, even why some of them are more quarrelsome and aggressive than others.

At any rate, here, in brief summary, are a few of the basic facts or possibilities about human behavior based on physical structure. The sooner you recognize and accept your child for what he is, the sooner you can help him to be a good whatever-it-is. The longer you delay such recognition, the more likely you are to waste effort and energy and even emotion in trying to push a child into being something that Nature never intended (and very likely will never permit.)

Physical Appearance

The child with the soft, rounded, well-padded body (whom Sheldon classes as an *endomorph*) may be expected to behave quite differently from the stocky, broad-shouldered, squarely built, well-muscled *mesomorph,* or from the thin, angular, flat-chested, and stoop-shouldered child with pipestem arms and legs whom we call an *ectomorph*.

In more detail (Sheldon, 41; Ames, 4), people of the three physical types differ as follows:

The body of the endomorph is round, soft, and well padded; of the mesomorph hard and square; of the ectomorph linear, fragile, delicate. In the endomorph, arms and legs are relatively short compared with the trunk, with the upper part of the arm longer than the lower part. Hands and feet are small and plump. Fingers are short and tapering. In the mesomorph, extremities are large and massive, with upper arm and leg equal to lower arm and leg in length. Hands and wrists are large, fingers squarish. In the ectomorph, arms and legs are long compared with the body, the lower arm longer than the upper arm. Hands and feet are slender, fingers are fragile with pointed fingertips. The endomorph tends to be short-waisted; the ectomorph long-waisted; while in the mesomorph the distance from waist to neck more or less equals the distance from waist to knees.

Knowing how endomorphs or mesomorphs or ectomorphs customarily behave, or are thought to behave, may help you fit your own expectations closer to reality than might otherwise be the case. Obviously, the more closely your expectations agree with reality, the happier and more comfortable both you and your child will be. Many parents find themselves quite ready and able to accept some less than ideal child behavior if they feel secure that this is the way their particular child may be expected to behave.

It is very important to keep in mind that most people do not fall entirely in one category or another. Most have some characteristics of each. But in most people one or the other tends to predominate. Thus for practical purposes we may speak roughly as if each child were of one type or another.

To begin with, it may be useful to you to know that, according to Sheldon, the endomorphic individual is one who attends and exercises *in order to eat*. Eating is his primary pleasure. The mesomorph, on the other hand, attends and eats *in order to exercise*. What he likes best is athletic activity and competitive action. The ectomorph, on the other hand, exercises (as little as possible) and eats (with indifference) *in order to attend*. Watching, listening, thinking about things, and being aware are his most enjoyable activities.

Sheldon gives another good clue to the differences among the three types. He says that when in trouble the endomorph seeks people, the mesomorph seeks activity, while the ectomorph withdraws and prefers to be by himself.

Children of the different physical types differ especially in their reaction to other people. The endormorph loves company. He is warm and friendly with others. He likes people and people like him. It is more important to him to have things go well than to have his own way. Other people tend to feel relaxed and comfortable when they are with him. He does not like to be alone.

The mesomorph, too, likes people, but he is nowhere near as dependent on their company as is the endomorph. However, he usually has plenty of friends and is a natural-born leader even in his preschool years. He likes people well enough, but as a rule other people have to adapt to *him*. He gets on best as a leader, the one the others look up to. He likes to command. And he likes others primarily because of the things they can do, because of the activities they can enjoy together.

The ectomorph, in contrast to the other two kinds of children, has a strong need for privacy. He likes to be alone and dislikes being socially involved. If he has a choice—which the young child does not always have—the ectomorph avoids being too much involved with other people. He tends to be distressed, uncomfortable, anxious, and shy in social relationships, as in nursery school, where he relates better to the teacher than to the other children.

How Children of Each Type Get Along with Siblings

So what does all of this suggest as to how children of each outstanding physical type may be expected to get along with brothers and sisters?

The child of *endomorphic* physique might be expected to be the most placid and amiable, the least easily aroused or irritated, the least competitive or combative. "Peace at any price" might be said to be his motto, though actually for him the price may not be too great, since getting on nicely with other people—at least most of the time—tends to be second nature.

He likes other people, enjoys their company, relishes good fellowship. Even at the naturally egocentric age of six years, when many children find it virtually impossible to lose gracefully when playing competitive table games, he may accept defeat rather graciously. The other player's goodwill may be more important to him than winning a game.

It is the endomorph who inquires touchingly, "Don't all children love their brothers and sisters?" In fact, it was a four-year-old endomorph who replied to her six-year-old brother's comment that he wished he didn't have a little sister and then he wouldn't have to share everything, with the calm observation, "But that's God's plan, Damon."

Interestingly enough, this is a two-way thing. The typical endomorph is so warm and friendly and affectionate that he tends to bring out the best in other people. He loves them and very often they love him in return, feel good in his presence.

Blessed in many respects are the parents of endomorphs. Those who have just endomorphs may wonder why all this fuss about children in a family not getting along with each other. (These parents of course are likely to be endomorphs themselves, which often makes for a very jolly and comfortable family.)

Now suppose one or more of your children is a *mesomorph*. The story will be very different indeed. Loud of voice, rough of manner, and noisy in action, this child may barge through his early years with all the grace of a bull in a china shop.

His own need to command and to win, combined with his customary lack of sensitivity to other people's feelings, make him a less than ideal playmate. So long as others follow his lead and play by his rules, all may be fine. Otherwise (unless play-mates are so much older and stronger that he sensibly obeys them) he tends to take offense and to become angry. When this occurs, he takes it out physically on playmates or siblings.

Since he himself may seem almost impervious to physical pain, and since he often doesn't seem to know his own strength, it is not unusual for him to do actual physical harm to brothers and sisters.

As a rule rather skilled at gross motor activities but often clumsy with his hands, he is apt to break the things he touches. And active as he is, he touches a lot. Not very sensitive about matters of ownership (unless he himself is the owner) he tends to get into, and to break or damage, many of his siblings' be-longings.

This quite naturally leads to objection on their part. Then he reacts and—wham!—the fight is on.

Quite obviously any child who is constantly active, "always on the go," and determined to dominate and command, will not bring out the best in brothers and sisters. In fact he will not even bring out the best in his parents. Parents and teachers of extreme mesomorphs soon learn that they just cannot react to every "bad" thing their child does. They will need to just plain not notice many things.

Siblings cannot be expected to show the same restraint. They tend to be all too ready to react. And do. Thus parents of a mesomorphic child often feel that if it were not for him, their family life would be much more peaceful than it usually is.

One further liability of mesomorphy is that, just as he is relatively impervious to pain, the mesomorphic child seems relatively unaware of subtle moral and ethical distinctions. Thus he very often behaves in a way that his parents and siblings alike consider "bad" and wrong. This stirs things up even further.

Here is our own answer to a mother concerned about the way her mesomorphic five-year-old treats his little brother. The mother writes as follows:

Dear Doctor Ames:

My husband's and my great concern, in fact mortal fear, is that our older boy, Cleve, aged five, will really harm his little brother, Billy. I don't mean just hurt him so that he cries. I mean really harm him seriously.

Cleve is a big, and we think handsome and well-built boy, and good at sports. But he is horrendously noisy and aggressive. In fact he is never still. Always ready for a fight, terribly combatative and competitive, stubborn, often really ugly. He deliberately invites confrontation—with parents, friends, and especially with his little brother.

The Nursery school teacher likes him and says he gets on very well, especially with the older children and especially if she makes very firm rules and allows no infraction. Is it our fault that he is so terrible at home? Do you think he might really harm Billy? Or are all boys like that?"

Dear Mother:

No, not all boys are like that, though many do behave in the same way your son does. He sounds, from what you say, as if he were the kind of child we call a mesomorph. Such boys do live to conquer. They invite and enjoy competition. They are by nature loud, rough, noisy, active. They love a good fight.

Some, if one is fortunate, as they grow older express their need to compete and conquer in competitive sports or later, as adults, they compete in their chosen field and often do turn out to be leaders, at work and in the community.

However, in some, the angry, aggressive, competitive drives do not mellow or turn constructive. Many actually do harm other people, brothers and sisters or people outside the family. This isn't very comforting to tell you but it is important not simply to trust to luck and hope for the best.

If in another year, say, Cleve continues to behave as he is now doing, you could at least try either individual psychotherapy for him, or family therapy for the whole family. This doesn't mean it is the family's fault that he behaves as he does. But family therapy might help you as a family help him control his aggressive drives.

In some instances, if in addition to being of a mesomorphic build a boy (or girl) is what one calls hyperactive, you're adding insult to injury. You can't change a person's build. But if overactivity is due to improper diet, that is something you can work on. In fact, that would be our first move with Cleve—take him to a good allergist and at least see if a changed diet might not make him more comfortable within himself and less angry and aggressive.

And now for the skinny, supersensitive *ectomorph,* who is quite something else again. Tending to be fully aware of and responsive to the usual ethical and moral values, this child much of the time tries to do what is "right."

The problem lies in the fact that he wants other people (especially siblings) to do what is right, as well. Though not domineering in the way of the mesomorph, who wants to lead and command, the typical ectomorph nevertheless tends to want siblings to do things according to his own version of the "right" way. In fact, often less physical and more cerebral than a mesomorphic sibling, the extreme ectomorph may even go so far as to want other people to *think* the right way.

The typical ectomorph lacks the warm love of human companionship of the endomorph and the strong drive toward leadership of the mesomorph. Thus though he may be highly responsive toward some one single, chosen friend, he lacks a need for other people—a need that often makes children of other physiques put up with quite a lot just for the sake of companionship.

The ectomorphic child may be even more protective of his "things" than are children of other physical types and even more upset when his possessions are disturbed or touched or, in some cases, even looked at.

Quite the opposite of the casual, "anything goes" endomorph, the ectomorph tends to be highly irritable. Sensitive as he is to small sights and sounds, this child may be highly upset by a sibling who is talking when he wants to read, or even breathing loudly, or tapping feet or fingers. One sometimes feels that the ectomorph, even more than others, might be happier if brothers and sisters could just disappear, leaving him in solitary peace.

And to make matters even more difficult, many an ectomorph seems to have the memory of an elephant. He tends to hold a grudge and may even vow *never* again to speak to an erring brother or sister.

Thus the ectomorph, though less noisy, aggressive, and destructive than a mesomorphic sibling, sometimes can be equally disruptive of family harmony. And this is the child who may know all too well how to hurt a sibling most. If a girl, she aims her words as her mesomorphic brother may aim his blows. Her snippy self-satisfaction may be trying to both parents and siblings.

Not All Children Grow Up on the Good Side of Life

Now, regardless of physical endowment, there is one thing common to children of all physical types that is, at the same time, a further source of individual differences. It has been established by Gesell and others to the satisfaction of all but the most extreme environmentalists that behavior in the human individual does develop in a patterned and rather highly predictable way.

However, it has also been established (4) that behavior does not necessarily improve or get "better" as the child matures. Rather, stages of equilibrium seem to alternate rather systematically with stages of disequilibrium. We think of this as a spiral of development, with changes from disequilibrium to equilibrium taking place at approximately six month interludes in the years between eighteen months and five years. The accompanying figure illustrates a more or less typical progression of age changes.

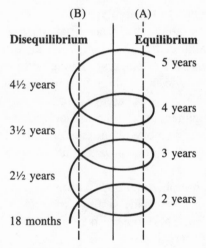

This, however, is just on the average. One of the more conspicuous aspects of individuality is related to the timing of the occurrence of these age changes. Some boys and girls are, on this spiral, ahead of the place which their chronological age might lead us to expect. They are, for instance, at three years of age already at the three-and-a-half-year stage of insecure disequilibrium. Others develop more slowly than average. For example, such children may, at the usually calm age of five, be merely at the customary four-and-a-half-year-old stage of disequilibrium.

A second large group of individual differences can be observed in relation to the place in the theoretical spiral where any given child's *midline* of behavior occurs. Say it should be displaced to the right of the position shown in the figure (see dotted line A). You would have a child whose behavior swings between extremely good and not quite as good, but the child might be expected always to be in reasonably good equilibrium.

Conversely, if a child's midline is displaced to the left (see dotted line B) behavior would swing between marked disequilibrium and moderate disequilibrium. But such a child's behavior might most of the time be more or less on the disequilibrium side of average.

Parents of children whose behavior tends always to be in rather good equilibrium are likely to take much of the credit for this good behavior. Parents of children whose behavior much of the time tends to be on the disequilibrium side of the spiral know to their sorrow that even the best of handling does not necessarily bring good results. This holds for brother-sister relationships as well as for any other kind of behavior.

Thus, obviously, though there does exist a rather standard and "typical" pattern of development, individual differences between and among children can be as marked as night and day.

What About That Boy or Girl Who Seems to Lack an Ethical Sense?

It is customary to blame parents when any boy or girl behaves consistently in what seems like a totally amoral manner, seemingly unable to distinguish right from wong.

Early, before seven years of age or so, many quite normal children seem able to distinguish right from wrong only by making lists for themselves as to what their parents permit or do not permit. Thus a six-year-old of our acquaintance (24) dictated the following list of "Things to Do" (i.e., good things) and "Things

Not to Do'' (bad things). Any sort of generalization about right and wrong was clearly at some distance in her future.

Things to Do:
1. Say "I think you are eating good things today."
2. Pleasant things are lovely to do:
   (a) Eat nicely.
   (b) Always say "please" and "thank you."
   (c) Always remember to say "Good morning, good afternoon, good evening."
3. Eat dinner by ourselves without having to be reminded.
4. Keep quiet and answer people when they are talking to you.
5. Keep clothes clean.
6. Keep watches going—wind them.
7. Go to bed at 7:30.
8. Wake up at 7:30.
9. When people are breaking things, tell them to stop.

Things Not to Do:
1. Not to say "I am not talking to you."
2. Not to say "Give it to me."
3. Not to say "Give me the biggest piece of anything."
4. Spill crumbs on floor.
   (a) Spill milk or water.
   (b) Get food on hands or face.
5. Set fires anywhere.
6. Pulling away from someone when they are doing something nice for you.
7. Slamming doors.
8. Don't tear books.
9. Shouldn't keep windows open when it rains.
10. Don't tear clothes.
11. Don't break windows.
12. Don't call people when they are busy.
13. Don't break armchairs.
14. Don't pinch people.

Or consider six-year-old Dennis, who lived in Ohio and was visiting his New Haven grandmother. She requested him not to step on ants. He explained that Mom and Dad said you could step on ants if you wanted to. Grandma said, "Well, not when you're visiting me." So Dennis concluded, "Ohio ants are bad but New Haven ants are good." Here was the beginning of a generalization, even though an inaccurate one.

But starting around seven, many boys and girls, approaching what Piaget calls the level of abstract thinking, do seem ready for some sort of generalization about what things are right, what things wrong. This, clearly—provided they are ready and willing to act on this knowledge—can improve the relations between siblings.

However, and here's the catch, some boys and girls seem to be born without the makings of a good ethical sense. Environmentalists would presumably say that it is the parents' fault when such a lack occurs. Our experience suggests the contrary—that there are some children who continue to behave in a largely amoral manner in spite of the efforts of good, capable, and otherwise effective parents.

The following report is from a mother, herself a child psychologist, whose ten-year-old son Mike, intelligent and handsome and extremely popular with both children and adults, nevertheless gave both parents and siblings a very hard time. This was partly because he was extremely vigorous and aggressive and partly because he seemed to lack the usual restraint of knowing what one should and should not do.

SCENE

Mike and his eight-year-old brother were chopping ice in the skating pond, putting the pieces by the side of the pond and then taking them up to the top of a little hill. This incident ended in disaster. Here are Mother's questions and Mike's responses:

MOTHER. What happened?

MIKE. Jeff took the biggest piece up the hill and broke it on purpose. At least I thought it was on purpose because of the way he grinned. So I said, "You did it on purpose. I warned you you shouldn'ta done it."

So I pushed him through the pool once, but he had boots on. Then I jumped to the other side and pushed him again. Just as he was halfway across he stepped on a piece of ice and slipped and he thought I pushed him, but I didn't. But I can understand why he thinks I pushed him.

Then I pushed him over again when he was walking to the door and I pushed him over to the front lawn and asked him why he did it.

He didn't answer, so I told him to answer and he said, "I bet you can't make me do anything you want me to," and then I said, "I bet I can; how much do you want to bet?" And he bet me a nickle and then I bet him a nickle that I could make him do whatever I want him to until Mommy comes home. So all this time we've been doing what I wanted to.

And that's the whole story. Unless you want to know what I wanted to do.

MOTHER. What did you want to do?

MIKE. All I did was put my hand over his mouth when he wouldn't be quiet. The kind of things I wanted to do was to have him lay down on the ground and be quiet.

After a while I asked him if he wanted to go in because he was so wet and he said "Yes" and so I said we can't. And later I asked him if he wanted to go in and he said "No" so I kind of forced him in.

Then I told him to stand up in the house. And when he didn't, I forced him to with his hands at his sides.

I did all this for a measly old nickel.

MOTHER. How did you feel about this whole episode?

MIKE. Not very good. I didn't feel very good about forcing him to do all the things; but he was the one who made the bet.

MOTHER. How did Jeff feel about the whole episode?

MIKE. Awful. I could tell by his actions. By his crying and hollering to let him *GO*.

MOTHER. What is my next question going to be?

MIKE. How should I be punished.

MOTHER. Should you be punished at all?

MIKE. No, I don't think so. Because he was the one who made the bet and it is his fault that he got hurt.

MOTHER. Don't you feel that there is anything else to it?

MIKE. I know I shouldn't have forced him so hard. And I wouldn't have had to if he had just done what I asked, which was nothing too hard.

MOTHER. Don't you have any responsibility here?

MIKE. Yes, the responsibility to teach Jeff that he should not make foolish bets. And the responsibility to lead a good example, which I didn't.

MOTHER. How should the whole thing be resolved?

MIKE. I think we both ought to say we're sorry and forget it. But I want him to remember . . . *(pause)* When do we eat?

MOTHER. So, what did you do wrong?

MIKE. I shouldn't have pushed him in the first place. Shouldn't have pushed him down on the front lawn. Shouldn't have forced him to lie down and be quiet. Shouldn't have forced him to go into the house. Shouldn't have forced him to stand up. Shouldn't have fought with him. *I know it was wrong. What I don't know is why it was wrong.*

So what do you do about this kind of child, and especially about his relations with siblings? Unfortunately you have to deal with him *where he is.* If he is still at the six-year-old level, merely memorizing things that are good and things that are bad without a real concept of *why,* then you will have to spend much time going over situations item by item. It might be most useful to do this before he goes to school, out to play, or visiting. This will be tiresome and time-consuming, but it may be needed. You can get a tremendous feeling of achievement and accomplishment if and when he finally grasps some simple abstraction, such as that we do not physically manhandle those smaller or weaker than ourselves.

Similarly, whenever unfortunate incidents do occur, you may, like the mother quoted above, have to take the culprit back over his behavior step by step.

Sometimes even that much-maligned medium, television, can serve to teach moral lessons. For the most part, violent as many programs may be, they do end up with the good people winning out over the bad.

Since most children, even up through the teens, do like to have their parents watch at least some programs with them, the examples of evil behavior can be discussed with them. Children tend to consider their parents overmoral, but they may accept a home truth more willingly if it is the television screen, and not merely the parent, that is making the point.

There are some seemingly amoral children who are merely very slow in the ethical department. Most of such children do catch up one day. But unfortunately some remain as morals-blind as others may be color-blind.

Such children not only tend to get into much trouble in the neighborhood, they can keep an entire household in turmoil. One such individual can destroy the harmony not only of brother-sister relationships but of the entire family. In such cases, your best bet may be the help of a qualified family therapist, as described in Chapter 10.

Sex Differences in Behavior

In family living, can one's daughters be expected to behave quite differently from one's sons? We can safely say yes.

Nowadays many experts argue that differences in behavior we observe between girls and boys are due chiefly to our expectations and the way we treat them.

Certainly there is no question but that our (or society's) expectations do influence, modulate, modify an individual's behavior. But in our opinion they do not determine it. Nature does that.

If you agree with our basic thesis that behavior is a function of structure, you have your answer. The bodies of boys obviously differ from those of girls. Though admittedly there are many exceptions (such as most ectomorphs, who regardless of sex tend to be thin and straight up and down, without major curves or obvious muscles), just the basic geometric shape of the two sexes is different.

Girls on the average are much higher in endomorphy (roundness) and lower in mesomorphy (square, strong massiveness) than are boys. Girls in general tend to be somewhat pear-shaped—narrow shoulders, wide rounded hips. Boys in general have strong necks and wide shoulders, then narrow down in the hip region.

Thus the typical (if we may use such a large generalization) feminine torso is triangular with the apex of the triangle at the top; the typical masculine form is triangular with the apex at the bottom.

Girls being on the average higher in endomorphy tend to be strong in those behaviors that theoretically characterize the typical endomorph. That is, they are emotionally friendly and easy to get along with, basically mothering and nurturing and understanding in relation to other people. Boys being on the average higher in mesomorphy are more active, vigorous, aggressive, competitive, eager to dominate and to rule.

Thus many of us conclude that our typical stereotypes of masculine as contrasted to feminine behavior have been developed from actually observed behavior rather than, as some contend, being merely our own biased projections.

Certainly any of us would urge that boys be permitted to express the gentler, girls the firmer or stronger, aspects of their natures without being criticized. But those child specialists who are in essence biologically oriented do believe that most girls are by nature rather "feminine"—with all that the word implies—and most boys to a large extent "masculine."

So what do these physical differences—if they are as characteristic and widespread as we believe—lead us to expect in the way of family relationships?

There are a number of exceptions, of course, but many parents do report that in general girls are easier to raise than boys and in general contribute less to family turmoil.

It is generally accepted that girls, on the average, develop more rapidly than boys. In a recent study of our own (6) we compared responses of children aged two-and-a-half to six years of age to the standard Gesell Preschool Tests. That is, we compared boys to girls with respect to the age at which they could copy forms (triangle, cross, square, etc.), build with small blocks, respond to a request to add usual parts to an unfinished drawing of a man.

In fifty-nine comparisons of ages at which a new behavior appeared, boys were ahead of girls in seven instances, the two sexes were equal in two instances, girls were ahead of boys in fifty.

Since little girls tend to be relatively more mature in their behavior than young boys, it stands to reason that if they are also by nature relatively more gentle, peace-loving, and people-oriented than boys, they may be expected to add more to family harmony and to create less turmoil and discussion than their brothers.

Certainly the almost incessant "wrassling" that sometimes goes on between two brothers is seen much less often between two sisters. Girls have their own ways of creating dissension within the family. They can be mean, snippy, and nasty. They slat their shoulders and toss their heads and argue and bitch. They may even scratch and pull hair. But in general they are not as outrightly physically aggressive in intersibling relationships as are their brothers.

The exceptions to these generalizations could fill a book, of course. But these are some of the more obvious and common differences between boys and girls in the family setting that we have noted ourselves and that parents have reported to us.

Can You Change Them?

Many people spend much of their lives trying to change (improve) those around them. Nowhere is this as true as in the parent-child relationship. And certainly it is true that, regardless of any child's basic and inborn physical structure, there are things one can do to help that child function more effectively.

To begin with, by providing activities that suit his aptitudes and inclinations, you can sometimes motivate your calm, relaxed, and usually happy endomorph toward expending just a little extra energy, spur him on to slightly more active accomplishment than would otherwise have been achieved.

You can sometimes, with much effort, calm down your ever-active, loud, and vigorous mesomorph. Or if not that, you can perhaps plan opportunities for him to expend some of his abundant energy outdoors, in approved athletic or other activity, rather than in the house, which offers so many booby traps for a child of this physique.

Your skinny, shy ectomorph will probably never become the life of the party, but you can try, especially while he is young, to provide minor and undemanding social activities that will lure him out of his shell. Being alone and reading may remain his favorite form of entertainment. But you can at least require some more active intermissions from this sedentary and solitary pleasure.

All these things you can do, but so far as we know, you cannot expect to change any person's basic temperament. If you are willing to accept this, it will save you countless days and weeks and even years of futile, frustrating effort and aggravation. Actually this holds true for spouses as well as for children. Most people behave as they do, much of the time, not simply to be aggravating or uncooperative, but because that is the way they are structured. And there is relatively little you can do to change that structure.

Summary

In short, every child is a unique individual and children differ tremendously one from the other. Some people believe that parents, by their handling, cause these differences, but almost any parent of more than one child knows from experience how very different each child is from all others, no matter how similarly or equally one tries to treat them.

In helping one's children to get along with each other, in helping to keep things harmonious, many of us have discovered that a good understanding of the basic personality and ways of reacting of each member of the family can be a tremendous help. Appreciation of the quality of each individual ingredient (family member) obviously helps us understand, and at least to some extent control, the mix when we get them together.

Keep in mind that some children just naturally behave nicely, get along with others easily, and tend to have a good understanding of what we adults consider right and wrong. Others find it more difficult to sense the feelings of others, to adapt to others, or to understand what it is that society considers right and wrong. As Sheldon discovered in his study of delinquency (42), the majority of his delinquents rated very high in mesomorphy, that is, in their level of physical activity. He also observed that mesomorphs in general often seem relatively unaware of subtle moral and ethical distinctions. They often need to be "taught" things that other children sense instinctively or pick up quickly.

However, though we ourselves believe that to a very large extent behavior is a function of the actual structure of the individual's body, it must inevitably also be influenced by those around him. Any child might be quite different from what he actually is if brought up in a family other than his own.

Chapter Seven
Families Have Personalities, Too

People, quite obviously, have personalities, but families have personalities, too. They range all the way from the gentle, friendly, happy family where much of the time children and parents get on with each other in harmony, to the extremely tempestuous, where shouting and yelling and actual physical violence may be the order of the day. There are families in which trips to the emergency ward are almost as frequent as trips to the supermarket.

Those parents who write (often very good) books about sibling relationships tend to picture themselves for the most part as extremely rational and reasonable, standing back from sibling quarrels till they seem to be getting really out of hand and then stepping in judiciously to pour oil on troubled waters. Or they make, and apparently enforce, good calm rules like "No hitting!"

It is important, if you are a parent in a violent household, not to think you are the only adult who sometimes loses control and not to blame yourself for all of your family's turmoil. The emotional climate of any family is multiply determined. Strong, vigorous, aggressive parents often (though certainly not always) produce strong, vigorous, aggressive children.

These children, then, interact violently, partly because of their basic inborn temperaments, partly because they are influenced by all the shouting and hitting they may see around them. And the whole thing tends to escalate. It can become a vicious circle.

We would not go so far as to defend violence in the household, but it is certainly true that a rather volatile family can absorb an amount of discord that might be quite distressing or even destroying to a calmer family.

Even a rather aggressive boy or girl, if he lives in a basically peaceful household, might curb his aggressiveness. On the other hand, even a fairly well-controlled boy or girl, surrounded by shouting and screaming and slapping people, may permit himself actions he would not commit if everyone were quiet.

Certainly any child's behavior is to some extent determined by the way people react to that behavior. Thus a child in a violent family might conceivably appreciate that his acts of verbal or physical violence were hardly noticed amid the general uproar.

Would this cause him to act up even more? Or would the lack of attention his behavior attracts discourage repetition? Who knows? Conversely, even a rather violent child, if a member of a calm and gentle family, might soon appreciate that his own acts of aggression were out of keeping and might soon subdue them. Or if he found he was "getting away with murder," might he not continue to do so? Again, who knows?

Happily, if either one of the parents or some one of the children is of a basically calm, kind, and gentle nature, he can often do a lot to keep things peaceful. And, as discussed in some detail in Chapter 9, there are some things that any family, no matter how unharmonious by nature, can do to make things more comfortable. Family living, no matter how difficult, can usually be improved if even one or two members of the family can act constructively.

Stern Father—Permissive Mother

One special family pattern, all too common and often more or less damaging, is that of the overfirm father and the overpermissive mother. For some reason this seems to have a more unfortunate effect on boys than on girls. At any rate, this kind of family setup often does produce young men, well endowed and from supposedly good home environments, who as adults come to difficulty either with the law or with their own emotions.

Every family tends to seek some kind of balance. In most, one or the other parent is the disciplinarian, the other the one who stands up for the children and tries to protect them and to see that they have privileges and advantages.

There are, of course, many exceptions, but as a rule it is the father who is firm, the mother who is permissive. Part of the reason for this lies in the fact that a mother is usually with the children longer hours than her husband and thus is more aware than he of their abilities and inabilities, their strong points and their weak ones.

As a consequence, it is more often Father than Mother who makes demanding statements: "It's time now that that child is toilet trained" . . . "It's time that he should dress himself" . . . "It's time now that she knows enough to tell the truth" . . . "It's time now that she learned to read."

A father's timetable tends to be arbitrary. He often just makes up his mind that now is the time for certain things to occur. A mother's is more modified by what she knows the children are and are not ready to do.

Whatever the reason, a balance is usually achieved. So long as parents don't quarrel in front of the children about matters of discipline, it is by no means harmful that one is stern, one more accepting. Children learn very quickly that with one parent they can get away with quite a lot, but that with the other they had best jump when they are spoken to.

But if these differences in handling are carried to extremes—a father overstern, a mother overpermissive—special personality problems do arise. Extremes of behavior often occur in families where the father is a hard-driving, success-oriented individual who actually does achieve outstanding triumphs in the outside world.

There are doubtless many other father/mother combinations that work against the child's best interests—but this is the one we see most often.

When Mother Works

One big difference in modern families is that which exists between those in which the mother is primarily a homemaker and does not work outside the home, and those in which Mother works whole or part-time (often in addition to homemaking).

Information is currently lacking on the amount of sibling quarreling that goes on in the two kinds of households. But our guess is that, since at least a portion of this quarreling is motivated by a wish to gain parental attention and approval—"You were right, Billy. Susan shouldn't have hit you"—there may actually be less quarreling in families where the mother works. (Of course the children can, and often do, telephone her about their quarrels and problems.)

The mother mentioned earlier who authored the telling comment, "Mother's home. Everybody cry!" was expressing something that really does happen. Mother, in most homes, seems to be the person everybody takes things out on. Many of us complain that our children behave better for almost anyone else but us—grandmother, aunt, even a teenage babysitter. But this is true because people other than Mother, especially baby-sitters, care less deeply about what goes on than mothers do. It isn't the baby-sitter whose approval Horace wants. It isn't the baby-sitter whom he is trying to get to punish or at least to criticize his little brother. It isn't the baby-sitter he wants to be first with. It is Mother.

So, if the quarreling is superficial and not resulting from a deep-seated hatred or rivalry, chances are that it occurs most when Mother is present.

As a result, in families where the mother works outside, there often is less quarreling than when she is at home full-time, simply because there is less payoff. But not always.

Most children react to the emotional atmosphere of the household, being themselves tense and irritable when the household is tense and irritable. Thus—as is often and understandably the case—a tired working mother, arriving home from work with her housework still to do, is at less than her best emotionally, and her tension often leads the children to react badly. Also, if each child is struggling for her attention, the less of it available, the more intense the struggle over how it is divided.

A further hazard is that some children, especially the very young, miss their working mother so much that even a naturally sunny and amiable child may become quarrelsome and difficult.

These negatives may be balanced by the positive fact, reported by many working mothers, that they feel so much better about themselves as persons that they have the patience and stamina to handle their children's quarrels. Also, simply being away from home regularly gives them a perspective that makes these quarrels loom less large. When Mother does not *care* quite so much, many children find that the thrill and satisfaction of quarreling diminishes.

So it could conceivably go either way. A mother's working away from home could make quarreling better or worse. Research is needed before anyone can say anything particularly solid in this respect, and such research would seem most difficult to set up or to carry out.

Still, with so many mothers employed either full- or part-time, it would be useful for us to know more than we do as to just what effect this working has on sibling relationships.

The Single Parent Family

A full-page ad in *The New York Times* recently described the two-parent family, with wage-earning dad, stay-at-home mom, and two kids, as the Great American Myth. The ad claims that this description fits only 7 percent of all American households. Not only does Mom not stay at home but often there is no Dad.

Seven percent seems low to us, but whatever the percentage, all of this is not exactly new. The single-parent family has always been with us, even though in times past it was more often caused by death or desertion than by divorce or intent. In fact, as Gardner points out (22), "There is nothing really new in the alternative life-styles that are being given so much publicity these days. There is no pattern that has not been tried many times over, somewhere, someplace, in mankind's long history."

For all the prevalence of one-parent families, solid information about the effect of this singleness on the children involved is surprisingly lacking. Thus we can only guess as to what effect this situation has on sibling relationships.

In family situations where great hardship exists, the children often develop extremely strong and close ties to each other. This could of course be true as well in a family of children lacking two parents.

In most instances, however, one must presume that sibling rivalry is as prevalent in a one-parent family as in the two-parent kind—and very possibly more prevalent, since the children would be vying for the affection and attention of only one person.

For the most part our advice to the single parent about sibling quarreling is pretty much what it is for the two-parent family—ignore, separate, be calm, display vast patience.

We would add the basic suggestion customarily given to the single parent. Don't try to do it all alone. Expand your family unit in any reasonable way you can. Add relatives, support groups, friends—especially friends of the opposite sex from your own, who can to some extent take the place of the absent parent.

Not every fatherless child will go as far as a little boy we saw recently who claimed that baseball player Reggie Jackson was his father. But all do have a natural wish and need to relate to grown-ups of both sexes. One thing that even the most effective single parent finds it hard to provide is a role model for the adult of the opposite sex.

The Stepfamily

And here's the big one—the question to which nobody we know of has the perfect answer: How do you manage, in a stepfamily, so that the children involved will get along comfortably with one another?

We know of no research that has even started looking for the answer. Even the numerous helpful books about stepfamily living—we especially recommend those by Roosevelt and Lofas (39) and by Emily and John Visher (50)—focus more on the parent-child relationship than on the way stepbrothers and stepsisters get on with each other.

The whole matter is so extremely complex and so fraught with hazard that we often wonder how anyone has the courage to blend two families of children in intimate everyday living. The possibilities for contention are almost infinite. But so, of course, are the possibilities for harmony and eventual good feeling.

Since the stepparent-and-child relationships are primary in establishing a harmonious new family situation, many stepparents spend much of their time and energy, at least in the early stages, in working out their own good relations with their new sons and daughters. How the children in the family get along may have to take second place, at least for a time.

It is hoped that suggestions in this book will be as useful to a stepfamily as to any other kind of family. But perhaps our chief suggestion to the new stepparent is to give your family at least a year to jell before you try to improve intersibling relationships.

Certainly you will do the ordinary things, make the ordinary moves and gestures, carry on the step-sibling relationship as you presumably have carried on earlier relationships among your own children.

In a crisis (and there will probably be many) you may need to zero in on the way the children in the family get along. But the best time to work seriously on such problems may have to wait until you have worked out the worst bugs of parent-stepchild relating. Not only is this relationship primary for family harmony, but obviously your effectiveness in improving sibling relationships depends heavily on how you yourself get along with the children.

For a while, it may seem like very tough going. But be encouraged. Many, many stepfamilies do make it to the point where family living in general—and brother-sister relationships in particular—becomes satisfactory and rewarding.

Chapter Eight

Is Your Home a Violent Place?

Violence in the American Family

Lest we sound too entirely negative in our description of the ordinary American home, it's only fair to note that there are households in which, much of the time, things go very smoothly indeed. For instance, we have seen homes in which the family consists of a soft-spoken mother and father and two gentle little girls, where peace and harmony prevailed. An occasional frown or tear or sulk or withdrawal to one's own room occurs—even a silent vow never to speak to a sibling again—but nothing major.

But in perhaps the majority of families, especially when the children are young, there tends to be quite a lot of confusion. Those parents whose children hit, kick, bite, or otherwise physically harm each other tend to worry not only that such scrapping will do permanent damage but also that it is unusual, atypical, or abnormal.

The first of these anxieties is a reasonable one. It is quite likely that siblings who are physically embroiled *will* harm each other. The second anxiety is less well founded. No matter what the level of physical combat in your family, it has most certainly been equaled or exceeded in many another.

Some of the most up-to-date, authoritative—and frightening—information about violence in an ordinary American home is described by Murray A. Straus (46) in his book *Behind Closed Doors: Violence in the American Family* and in other scientific reports by him and his colleagues (26, 44, 45). What Straus has to report is not good news, but it may serve to console you that the violence in your own family is at least no worse than the violence in others.

Straus and his colleagues compiled annual rates of violence in a group they regarded as representative of American families. They found that in 16 percent of these families, there were physical acts of violence between spouses; with about the same frequency, children attacked their parents; in more than 63 percent of the families, parents attacked their children. Table 1 on page 171 gives this information in tabular form.

But, according to Straus, the most frequently occurring type of family violence is attacks by one of the children against a brother or sister.

This is so common that some parents worry if it does not happen. "Kids will fight" as they say. And indeed they do. Eight out of ten American children get into a physical fight with a sibling each year. But this is even more likely to be an underestimate than the other rates because there are certain to have been fights the parent did not know about.

Not only are children more violent to each other than to anyone else, in addition, they are the ones most likely to attack in ways that could cause serious injury. Over half of American children do one or more of the following to a sibling each year: kick, bite, punch, hit with object, beat up, or attack with a knife or gun.

As children grow older their violence rate goes down, but it far from disappears. Taking just the major acts of violence, the annual rates go from 74 per hundred three- and four-year-olds, to 64 per hundred five- to nine-year-olds, to 47 per hundred 10- to 14-year-olds and 36 out of every hundred 15- to 17-year olds.

These statistics and much other data suggest that the family is the most physically violent group or institution that a typical citizen is likely to encounter. Ironically, the family is also the most loving and supportive group or institution as well. That fact, says Straus, has blinded us from seeing the violent side of family life. In fact, it would almost seem that the family is the place where most of us learn to be violent.

It is true that most parents do try to stop physical fights and to teach children not to hit their brothers and sisters. However, most adopt the theory that violence within the family is just a part of life—not necessarily a good part but one that is to be expected. Says Straus:

> Parents react differently than if it was *someone else's* child who had been punched or kicked by one of their children, or *someone else's* child who had done that to one of their children. If it is someone else's child, there would be cries of outrage, and possibly even legal action if the violence persisted. But between their own children, parents, in effect, tolerate such behavior for years. The data from our research show that the same children are far more violent to their own siblings than they are to other children. Moreover, this continues into the late teen ages. In one of our samples, 62% of the high school seniors hit a sibling during the year, but "only" 35% had hit someone outside the family during that same year.

He continues:

> Conflict in the family is also high because, unlike special purpose groups (such as academic departments, universities, or factories) the activities and interests of a family cover just about everything. Hence there are more things to get into a hassle about . . . more "events" over which a dispute can develop than is true for other groups.

Neither Straus nor we can offer a foolproof remedy for all of this violence. But Straus does suggest that any parent who may have been so inclined should make every effort not to spank his children or in fact not to inflict any form of physical punishment.

> Physical punishment is the foundation on which the edifice of family violence rests. It is the way most people first experience violence and it establishes the emotional content of associating love with violence. The child learns early that those who love him or her are also those who hit. Since physical punishment is used to train the child or to teach him about dangerous things to be avoided, it establishes the moral rightness of hitting family members.

How Do Siblings Influence Each Other's Behavior?

It is interesting and possibly helpful to parents to know how boys and girls other than their own behave in relation to each other. The most objective information we know of has been supplied by Sutton-Smith in *The Siblings* (47). He questioned fifth- and sixth-grade boys and girls, asking them specifically whether or not, in getting siblings to do what they want them to, they used certain listed techniques. They were asked to score these items on a five-point scale, ranging from 1 for "Never" to 5 for "Always." Thus, obviously, the higher the score the more often the behavior in question occurred.

A second, similar, questionnaire scored the frequency, as reported by the boys and girls, of different techniques that siblings used to get *them* to do what the siblings wanted.

In reporting Sutton-Smith's findings, we have taken the liberty of grouping these techniques into the following categories: violent actions, verbal efforts, asking for help, emotional response, and a final category that we call miscellaneous.

The findings also indicate which brother-sister (brother-brother/sister-sister) combinations most frequently perform each kind of behavior. The tables on which the following discussion is based can be found on pages 172 through 175.

Negative intersibling interaction seems to appear in any and all sibling combinations.

Regardless of the particular sibling relationship, the children report the following to be the most frequently occurring violent actions: beat him up; scratch, pinch, pull hair, bite; tickle; wrestle, sit on, chase; attack things (hide toys, spoil bed); threaten to hurt; stop from using things (phone, bathroom, toys); lock out of room.

Verbal efforts to influence siblings included bossing but also promises, bribes, and simple requests. Perhaps because more approved of by parents, these are used more frequently than physical violence. Asking parents for help with intersibling problems is a customary way of achieving sibling compliance; emotional efforts, such as getting angry (shouting, screaming, yelling, getting mad) or spooking them, are a bit less frequent.

As to the sibling relationships, we note that the three combinations where violence occurs most are as follows: a girl with a younger sister, a girl with an older sister, and a boy with an older brother.

As to verbal ways of getting a sibling to do what one wants him to, the following sibling combinations lead: a boy with a younger brother, followed in lesser frequency by a girl with an older sister, a girl with a younger sister, and a boy with an older brother.

As to emotional ways of getting siblings to do what one wants, the following sibling combinations lead: a girl with an older sister, a girl with a younger sister, and a boy with an older brother.

Thus a girl with an older sister is a leading activator of violent, verbal, and emotionally attacking activities.

A girl with an older brother seems least likely to use either violent physical, verbal, or emotional ways of getting a sibling to do what she wants him to.

As to ways in which young people report that their siblings get them to do what they (the siblings) want them to, findings are not too different. Of violent actions which rate 2.5 or more on a scale of 1 (Never) to 5 (always), the following are reported:

beat up, belt, hit; scratch, pinch, pull hair, bite; tickle; wrestle, sit on, chase; attack things; threaten to hurt; lock out of room.

Verbal efforts include primarily the following: promise them things; boss—say "Do it," "Shut up"; bribe or blackmail; ask them; flatter them; bargain; tell tales; explain, reason, persuade; tease, call names, or pester; threaten to tell.

Asking parents for help in getting siblings to comply is for most a useful technique. Emotional efforts include most of all getting angry (shouting, screaming, yelling); crying, pouting, or sulking; making sibling feel guilty.

As to kinds of sibling relationship in which these methods are used most, vigorous if not violent ways of being treated by siblings seem to run through all possible sibling combinations. However, here, too, the least unfriendly interactions seem to occur between girls and their older brothers.

Comment

Straus and Sutton-Smith come up with slightly different figures as to who does what to whom under what circumstances and how often, but both clearly find that there is a good deal more kicking, hitting, pinching, hair pulling, and other forms of physical violence—not to mention verbal and emotional attack—between siblings than most of us would like to believe.

If in your own household these things do not occur, count yourself lucky rather than skillful. If they do occur, at least be assured that you are by no means the exception.

Chapter Nine

Helping Your Child to Be Happier

It seems important for parents to have in mind some basic game plan—at least a few ideas as to what they will do when their children quarrel. You may choose, as most child specialists recommend, to ignore as much of their disagreement as you possibly can. You may choose to step in and separate them. You may use the popular Time Out method for whichever child you think would best be removed from the scene. Or you may resort to some more formal method of handling—and, it is hoped, preventing—disagreement.

However, quite obviously, your whole family would be better off if, instead of waiting till discord occurs and then dealing with it, you could somehow manage to live as a family in such a way that less bickering, quarreling, or outright physical fighting would occur.

Here are a few things you might do, or avoid doing, to make things happier and smoother for your children.

An Ounce of Prevention

Many a parent has commented to us, "I think they fight because they can't think of anything else to do." This is sometimes the case. Brothers and sisters fight partly because they really have things to disagree about. They fight partly because they enjoy it. But they also sometimes fight because they can't think of anything else to do.

There are numerous avenues to prevention. One of the best, as we have mentioned, is separation. This does not mean artificial, forced, unrealistic separation. It merely means planning your children's lives so that they are not constantly together.

When they are very young, staggering naps can help. Of course some mothers prefer to have all children nap at once because it gives them a brief breathing space. But separate naptimes can provide at least a few hours a day when children are not entangled.

Your best bet with the very young, especially with the preschooler who can't get along with siblings of a near age, is to send him to nursery school. It isn't that nursery school teaches children not to fight. It is that school can give them an emotional focus. It can enrich a child's life to the extent that he may no longer need the emotional satisfaction of fighting with siblings, not eating his meals, disobeying his mother.

If nursery school is successful—and it usually is—it can become a dominant interest in the life of a child, giving him a life of his own. "School tomorrow?" he will ask eagerly, if school is every other day. What his teacher says, does, wants, wears will be of major concern. His friends at school occupy many of his thoughts. That he wore a lion costume to the school party at Halloween is something he likes to think about.

And school, even though it does not exactly teach the child not to fight, does help him to get on better with other children. Preschoolers tend to find it difficult either to share or to take turns. A good nursery school teacher is very skillful in encouraging both of these behaviors.

She does it by telling a child reluctant to part with some prized toy or possession, "When you're finished, Johnny wants that shovel" . . . "Pretty soon it will be Jane's turn to play with the bike" . . . "Mary needs that truck" . . . "What else could you play with?'' With two-and-a-half year olds, considerable teacher encouragement is usually needed to achieve any sharing or giving up. But by three, many children will themselves make use of these very techniques, offering a grabber some alternative toy or other object or even giving up a toy that some other child may want.

An added advantage of nursery school is that many preschoolers discover at school, as they may not have found out at home, that they are *not* the center of the universe. In friendly fashion, a teacher can often encourage a child to believe, in a way that a mother may find hard to do, that he is only one among many people in the world. Also, relating to a teacher can help the child to spread out beyond the adults in his own family.

Admittedly not every preschooler, at every age, enjoys or adapts well to nursery school, but the majority do. And most parents accept its value. An amusing exception is Raymond Moore, who (36) feels that ''even a few hours a week in nursery school dilute your child's attachment to you and cause him to latch onto the values of his peers. Then your values get the back of his little hand. . . . Association with anyone other than a child's family is not normally required in the preschool years.''

Moore aside, we at Gesell—perhaps feeling more secure than he about the influence of our values—strongly recommend nursery school attendance for an unhappy or quarrelsome preschooler as well as for the happy and well-adjusted young boy or girl. We have found that the child happy and enthusiastic about this wonderful activity will have less need to fill his life with the dubious pleasure of fighting with a sibling.

A little later on, if staggered primary school schedules are available, their different hours of attendance may help keep young siblings apart. Play with neighborhood friends also helps. Time spent at other people's houses reduces time together, and even when playmates are brought home, a child and his friend often play in other parts of the house or yard from that occupied by siblings.

Still later, the children, one at a time, can spend longer periods away from home—and each other. An overnight with a friend will help. If willing relatives are available, a weekend at an aunt's or uncle's or grandparent's can work wonders. (These arrangements work especially well if you have only two in your family.)

It isn't just physical separation that one needs to aim for. Two or more children can be in the same house at the same time and still not necessarily in each others' hair. It is separate interests that are needed. The more interests a young person has, the more he learns to think of himself as a separate person, the less need he will have to be entangled with siblings.

Feedback

One of the most widely recommended ways of making your children feel good about themselves is effective communication with you—often referred to as feedback. This technique can be especially useful in allowing them to discuss with you their feelings about a brother or sister.

Free communication between children and parents is generally accepted as a desirable thing. But there are differences of opinion as to how to attain it. Some believe that if a child wants to talk with you, you should—if at all possible—stop what you are doing and give him your full attention. Others find it easier to communicate if the confrontation is not too direct, if you go on with what you are doing (washing dishes, painting woodwork, carpentering) and merely show by what you say that you are listening with interest.

Differences of opinion also exist among specialists as to what you should say. Some feel that if your son should tell you, "I really hate Billy" (his brother), or "You always take Billy's side," you should parrot back what he has said to you: "Oh! You feel that you hate Billy?" or "You think I always take Billy's side?" Others find that this kind of response tends to irritate some children, who then respond angrily, "That's what I *said!*" This group prefers a response such as, "Why don't you tell me about it?" (The conversation will then presumably proceed from there without further help from us.)

At any rate, it seems helpful to let any child get his feelings off his chest and to let him know that you really care about how he feels. And you can probably work some constructive advice or suggestions into the conversation.

Dodson, in his book *How to Grandparent* (17), gives what seem like good suggestions about conversations you may hold with your boy or girl.

He advises that you talk *with* your children, not *at* them.

Try not to be judgmental. If your son tells you, "I think Billy is a real twirp," don't say at once, "That's no way to talk about your brother." If your child knows you're going to be judgmental, chances are he won't talk to you very much.

Don't deny your child's feelings. If your daughter tells you about some little problem that bothers her, don't cut her off with "Surely, that little problem can't still be bothering you." (If it weren't bothering her, she wouldn't still be talking about it.)

Don't give false reassurance. Don't guarantee that things will all work out okay unless you're really sure. (And how often can you be really sure?)

Try very hard not to hand your child a free, gift-wrapped solution for all of his problems. Thus don't say, "Listen, here's what I would do about Billy's taking your things." (You're not your child, and your glib solution may not at all suit his way of doing things.)

When you can, avoid lecturing. Especially avoid lecturing that emphasizes how beautifully you handled a similar situation when you were young.

Don't attack with questions: "Okay, now let's be honest. What did you do to Janice to provoke her into tearing up your paper?"

Try not to moralize: "I think you should just make up and forget that the whole thing ever happened."

Don't threaten: "Look, I'm telling you for the last time. You tease your sister once more, and you'll wish you were in outer space."

Don't play amateur psychologist: "I think your whole problem is that you're just plain jealous of Jennie. That's why you do all these foolish things."

Above all, try to be brief in your own comments. Most grown-ups are much too long-winded with children. As one child put it: "Daddy, why do you give such long answers when I ask you such short questions?"

Now on the more positive side, Dodson suggests the following:

Take a physical stance that sends your child the message that you are actively listening to him. Don't try to dust or watch TV or repair your fishing tackle. When you and he are talking, maintain eye-to-eye contact that lets him know you are really concentrating on what he has to say.

Interject comments into the conversation that will keep your child talking, such as, "Tell me more about those feelings that it wasn't going to work out."

Try to talk to one child at a time. Dinner-table conversation is fine, but if you want your child to open up, best to get him alone.

Be brief when you respond. He will probably be more interested in what he is telling you than in what you have to say about it.

Grant your child genuine respect as a small human being. You have only to listen to parents talking to children in stores, at playgrounds, and at home to realize how few parents give their children this kind of respect.

Have the courage to disclose yourself as a real person with human feelings and weaknesses. If you have the courage to disclose these things to your child, it will do wonders for both of you. Also, research shows that when one person makes a disclosure to another, the second person usually makes a reciprocal disclosure. And when we disclose our feelings and weaknesses to our children, it enhances their self-confidence and helps them to realize they can succeed in spite of their fears and weaknesses.

Health

Many of the suggestions in this book will not be new to you. Many, indeed, will be things you have already tried for yourselves. However, there is one relatively new notion about child behavior that is only now being accepted even by many professionals in the field.

This is that a child's behavior, as well as his health, can be directly affected by foods eaten and by other things in the environment to which he has an allergic reaction.

Many years ago, Ilg suggested to parents that children who adamantly refused certain foods might perhaps be suffering from a minimal but undiscovered allergic reaction to that food or other substance—a reaction that not only made the child uncomfortable but might actually influence his behavior adversely.

In more recent times, other respected physicians, among them Wunderlich, Smith (43), Crook (13), Rapp, and Feingold (19), contend that either foods or inhalants to which a child is allergic can influence behavior as well as physical health.

As Rapp has put it (38):

When we think about allergy, we usually conjure up an image of sneezing, runny noses; itchy, tearing eyes; wheezing and coughing; or rashes. Less commonly recognized symptoms include muscle aches, headaches, dizziness, fatigue.

What about children who are often depressed or irritable, overly active, belligerent, or poor learners? You may know, or be the parent of, a child who is hard to discipline, continually disruptive, and *barely accepted by peers and siblings* because of hostile and erratic behavior. Some allergists and pediatricians believe these symptoms, also, can be due to allergies.

The literature on hyperactive (or so-called hyperkinetic) children is extensive. Among the behavior characteristics commonly associated with such children are the following: They are commonly found to be excitable and impulsive, restless, destructive, sensitive, bullying, cruel, immature, distractable, moody, easily frustrated, disturbing of others, boastful, and bragging.

Small wonder that such a child finds it difficult to get on with siblings, or that his siblings find it hard to get along with him.

It would be simplistic to assume that all the problems of brothers and sisters fighting with each other could be cured just by feeding everybody a proper diet and taking care of all allergies. But it is common sense to acknowledge that a healthy child is more likely to be a happy child than one who is suffering from severe allergic symptoms. And it is common sense to assume that a happy child will have less need to engage himself in quarrels with brothers and sisters than an unhappy, uncomfortable child.

Not every pediatrician is competent to help you with your child's diet and allergies, but it should be possible to find a physician who will help you help your child toward improved health and a reduction of allergic symptoms. References given on pages 179 to 181 suggest good places to start in attempting to learn how to protect your children from foods and inhalants that may be causing not only illness but problem behavior, as well as how to provide proper vitamin supplements to their diet.

Education

A child's success in school, or his lack of success, may seem somewhat remote from the way he gets along with brothers and sisters, yet it can have a very close relationship.

One of the basic contentions of the Gesell Institute is that children should be started in school, and subsequently promoted, on the basis of behavior age rather than chronological age or I.Q. As explained by Ames (2), behavior age means just what it sounds like. It means the age at which a child, as a total individual, is behaving.

Thus a child could be seven years old, yet if in general ways he is behaving like a five-year-old, he belongs in kindergarten with other five-year-olds, not in second grade where the law in many states would place him. We believe that perhaps at least 50 percent of school failures could be prevented or remedied by having each child in the grade for which developmental, or behavior, level suits him.

It is hoped that this proper fit will be taken care of before the child starts school, but if it hasn't been, and the child ends up in a grade for which his general level of performance doesn't suit him (he can't sit still, can't wait his turn, can't do those general things that the rest of the class can do), we maintain that he should be allowed to repeat a grade. Some parents worry that putting a child back a year might harm him emotionally, but our experience has been that the effect is, in nearly every case, extremely favorable.

What parents and teachers alike tell us is that not only does school performance improve after the child repeats, but personality is also affected favorably. Parents report—with almost monotonous repetition—"She's a changed child" . . . "He's a different boy" . . . "Now he goes around the house singing" . . . "It's as if the weight of the world were lifted off her shoulders."

And they supplement these encomiums with such further descriptions as "Now he has loads of friends" . . . "Now she's not so snippy and snarly" . . . "Now she gets on better with her brother and sister." It seems a logical progression: more success in school, increased feeling of self-worth, less tension and anxiety, better interpersonal relations.

Your Inner Child of the Past

Your hated little brother! Your bossy older sister! Do they still linger strongly in your memory? And do they actually influence your treatment of your own children?

Psychologist W. Hugh Missildine (35) maintains that our child-hood, in an actual, literal sense, exists within us even when we are adults, and affects everything we do and feel. According to Missildine, "Each of us carries within him his inner child of the past—a set of feelings and attitudes brought over from child-hood."

One of the greatest dangers of this is that as parents we may be influenced in our reactions to our own children by things that happened to us when we were young.

Say that you, a mother, were very much browbeaten and mis-treated (as you remember it) by your brother. This could cause you, as a parent, to identify with your daughter and feel resent-ment and hostility toward your son. It could result in your taking your daughter's part, whether she is in the right or not. It could lead to gross unfairness.

In fact, this kind of reaction can last over into a second gen-eration. We know of a grandmother who identified strongly with her granddaughter and saw in her grandson her own long-dead brother, who had bullied her when they were children. Whenever her grandchildren quarreled, she felt very angry, and it seemed to her that her granddaughter was always blameless, her grandson always the aggressor.

She would actually say to her own daughter (with whom she fortunately had a good relationship), "Are you going to let him get away with that?" Her daughter, who had an especially soft spot in her heart for her son, would reply calmly, "Yes, I am." So Grandmother remained angry.

(It is especially hard for a grandparent when it seems that one grandchild is consistently unfair and unfriendly to his siblings. There is relatively little that can be done about it. Having a thorough talk with the offender usually doesn't get far. Nor does discussing the matter with the child's parents, since they either do not think a problem exists or are already doing whatever they can about it. As a rule, the best that grandparents can do is to invite the "victim" to spend time visiting them. This won't solve the basic problem, but it can at least provide a pleasant interlude for the boy or girl in question.)

To sum up, even if you do your best, not all of your children will be well behaved and happy all of the time. Two of the main tasks of childhood are (a) growing up and getting free of parents and (b) learning to get on with brothers and sisters. Neither task is accomplished easily.

But the things discussed in this chapter may help. Sending a preschooler to nursery school can be the best gift you ever gave him. Nursery school, unless it is rigid and academically oriented, can be one of the happiest and most comfortable school experiences of a child's life.

Establishing good communication with your children, during the preschool years and ever after, is another big step toward improving their lives. Keeping up their health is another big contribution you can make. Seeing that your children are properly placed and thus, it is hoped, successful in school may also help.

And lastly, if you can avoid reacting to your children on the basis of remembered difficulties of your own childhood, you are on your way toward treating them more fairly and objectively than if your handling is all fuzzed up by your own childhood unhappiness.

A basically happy home atmosphere for your family, if you can provide it, can go farther toward preventing the usual bickering and quarreling than any set of rules, any special type of discipline. Some say that the best thing a husband or wife can do for the children is to try to make the other parent happy.

Chapter Ten

Formal Ways of Improving Family Relationships

Ideally, most parents should be happily married, should have produced healthy and well-adjusted and good-tempered children, and their family lives should proceed in a basically comfortable manner.

Unfortunately this natural, happy flow of living is by no means always the case. Many of our homes are rather violent places. Some parents consider violence and discord a normal part of living.

The Family Contract

Some families take rather formal steps to improve matters. One such approach is the so-called family contract. This has been best described by the Calladines (11), who have found that making contracts is one of the best ways to teach sibling consideration and to reduce rivalry and fighting. Parents can begin to teach the concept of contracts to even very young children.

Before entering into a contract, some basic rules should be set

out. Children should not be expected to share all toys and possessions, especially their favorites. Second, if a child does harm
a sibling's things, he is responsible for remedying the damage.
But the owner has some responsibility, too. He should if possible
keep his things in a reasonably safe place.

Here are some of the Calladines' rules for successful contracting:

1. Be clear on the purpose of the contract. It should be limited
to one specific situation, cover only one definable piece of behavior.

2. Allow time for good discussion before signing anything.

3. The contract should be put in writing. This will eliminate
later fuzziness about what it actually was that the children agreed
on.

4. Date the contract and provide a renewal or reevaluation
opportunity.

5. The actual signing of the contract is important. Children
value their signatures, the mark of their name. (They can sign
with an X or scribble before they are actually able to make their
name.)

6. And finally, post the contract in clear view.

You will probably find, if you do try contracting, that a formal
contract helps your children to understand the meaning of com-
promise. "If you'll get a pair of socks for me, I'll shoot a few
baskets with you." "I'll let you look at my trading cards if you'll
let me use your yo-yo." Thus after formal contracting over important things, many brothers and sisters find that they can, much
of the time, merely bargain verbally. If you as a family could
reduce the amount of quarreling by even 50 percent, it would be
well worth your trouble.

Family Council

A family contract, or for that matter a series of family contracts,
seems to us a very sensible way to make things more harmonious

within a household. An alternate, or supportive effort, is the so-called family council. Though this concept has received a good deal of publicity and promotion, to many it seems unrealistic and even undesirable. To many quite sincere parents, the picture of a whole family sitting down together at regular intervals for good, frank, sincere, and serious talks about how each one feels about the others' behavior, seems hazardous in the extreme.

There are families even today in which Father's word is law and where any frank and sincere criticism of his way of running the family would be met with rather severe retribution. Even in families where either or both parents are less arbitrary, there are apt to be repercussions in the wake of any excessive frankness.

Only you can tell whether or not yours is the kind of family that would welcome and benefit from a family council. One of the strongest exponents of the family council is the late Dr. Rudolf Dreikurs, who in a book with the hopeful title *Family Council: The Dreikurs Technique for Putting an End to War Between Parents and Children and Between Children and Children* (18) provides what he calls "The complete and authoritative guide to setting up, maintaining and operating a Family Council in the home."

Roughly (and our guess is that things could get very rough) it works like this. Dreikurs' position is that "Only as equals can we function in a democracy, and in the family situation, adults should be willing to accept a status of equality with their children." He describes the Family Council as a "way for family members to enjoy one another as people; a way to achieve mutual equality and respect."

According to him a Family Council consists of any group of people living together. He advises that they have regularly scheduled meetings and work under rules agreed on in advance. All concerned should feel free to say whatever they believe or feel, without fear of consequences. All must agree on any course of action before it is undertaken or followed up.

As Dreikurs envisions it, the Family Council is not merely

getting together and talking. It is a whole method for achieving democratic participation in the solution of common tasks and problems. *All members of the family are considered equal partners.*

If it sounds like your kind of thing, more power to you. If you find it unrealistic, however, other techniques, possibly more plausible, are available.

Behavior Modification

A new technique, extremely structured but rather popular, is called Behavior Modification. The philosophy behind it is that you can get almost anybody to do almost anything you want by *rewarding* acceptable behavior and *ignoring* behavior you wish to discourage.

In order to do this successfully, a parent should choose just *one* bad habit to work on at a time. A vague "getting Jim to be nicer to his younger sister" is too large and generalized a concept. Instead, pick out something specific. Say that Jim hits his sister whenever he gets angry at her, and you want him to keep his hands off her. So you make a *rule:* Whenever he plays nicely with her for, say (to begin with), ten minutes at a time, without hitting, he will be rewarded in some way. You and Jim should both agree on the reward. Keep a chart indicating successes. You will soon find that you can increase the specified time from ten minutes to fifteen or even more. (The child whose behavior you are trying to improve should of course be consulted about this change in time.)

And now comes the hard part, the reason that some parents find it so difficult to practice Behavior Modification. You are supposed to ignore the bad or undesirable behavior. (In this instance, if Jim does hit his sister, don't scold or punish; merely separate the children with as little comment as possible.) Ignoring bad behavior is very difficult for most parents. It is also confusing for the child, who at first may perform the undesirable activity more than ever. However, if it is consistently unnoticed (even scolding or punishing are of course a reward in that they are attention) the theory is that it will soon drop out.

Though you are not supposed to use punishment, even for quite bad behaviors, it is permissible to use what used to be called "Go to your room" and now is called "Time Out."

Graubard, in his practical book *Positive Parenthood* (25), gives three simple steps to be followed in using Behavior Modification with your children.

First, *identify* the behavior to be modified. In this case, it is Jim's hitting his sister. Since the behavior is one to be decreased, choose another behavior that you wish to increase (playing with her nicely without hitting for a specified period of time). Make the *rule* that if he does play nicely, he will be rewarded.

Second, *intervene* by reinforcing the desired behavior. You do this by providing the promised reward. This reward might not come *every* time Jim plays nicely for ten minutes. You might have made the rule that you will give him a mark on a chart for every specified period of good behavior, and the reward could come after a certain number of marks have been checked off. (Charting seems very popular with behavior modifiers. It shows how things are going.)

Third, *evaluate*. Your chart or record will help you do this. Then if things are not working out, you will have to reevaluate your plan. You can ask yourself: 1. Is my goal justified? 2. Is my goal specific and realistic? 3. Are there situational problems that must be solved first before my plan can be expected to work?

One further possibility offered by Graubard seems interesting. Though he feels, as we do, that in general one does best not to intervene when children are fighting, he suggests that if you feel you must step in, you might set up an incentive program along Behavior Modification lines *between the children*. Try to teach them that they can change each other's behavior by selectively ignoring and reinforcing. (Admittedly, ignoring is hardly new.

Our own parents used to tell us, "Just ignore him. Don't give him the satisfaction of noticing." But reinforcement is somewhat new.)

Thus if Johnny consistently provokes Mary, offer rewards. Johnny gets a reward if for some set period of time he does not provoke Mary. Mary gets the reward if she ignores the provoking.

You may need to narrow things down rather more than this. "Provoking" may be a too large and disputable term. You may need to identify the kind of provocation you are talking about: hitting Mary, disturbing her things, calling her names, for instance. And you may also have to identify the length of time you are talking about before the reward would be given.

When parents first hear about Behavior Modification, it often seems not too practical to them. The whole thing may seem self-conscious and hard work. The charting may seem time-consuming. And not punishing for bad behavior may seem nigh impossible. And yet, the more you read about it, and the longer you try it, the more interesting and plausible it may become to you.

Exponents of Behavior Modification, as for instance Roger W. McIntire (34), emphasize the importance of not making too many rules and not working on too many different problems at once, since any rule specifying a consequence takes time to carry out.

Also it is important, once you have learned not to scold and nag about a behavior, to avoid letting the child know in some nonverbal way when you are displeased. For example, as McIntire comments, "Looking upset or glaring are common substitutes for talk, but even these give the child *attention* for doing wrong." And that is a thing you want to avoid. Ideally, undesirable behavior should get no attention at all.

Family Therapy

So far so good. But let's say you have tried "everything": family contract, Family Council, Behavior Modification, or just the usual methods of preaching, praying, punishing, scolding, nagging, rewarding, supervising, separating—whatever comes natural to you. And none of them seem to work. Your house is a bedlam and your children still fight, as so many parents tell us, "constantly."

It is probably time now for outside help. Fortunately these days in many communities, very skilled outside help *is* available (Zuk, 52), in the form of a more or less new technique called Family Therapy.

Family therapy is different from conventional therapy. The latter deals with an isolated individual, and the therapist rarely comes right out and advises the patient specifically what to do. In family therapy intervention has shifted from attempting to change the individual in isolation, to helping the "identified patient" by changing the entire family system in which that individual lives.

The family therapist believes that family members often relate to each other in abnormal, harmful ways. For instance, the mother and children may form a coalition against the father. Or one sibling, posing to the parents as the "angel" of the family, may actually be the most hostile and most destructive member of the group.

Or family members may punish each other in their own strange ways. A mother may play the role of martyr or intermediary between the father and children, feeling sorry for herself as she does so, but actually gaining power and satisfaction in the process. Fighting between siblings may serve a quite different purpose, and may stem from a quite different motivation, than appears on the surface.

Such abnormal and unsatisfactory ways of relating may have become so ingrained and customary that families do not even realize what they are doing. In family therapy, then, not just the person or persons supposedly in trouble but the whole family takes part in the therapy process. The therapist brings their ways of relating into the open and actually takes sides, judiciously, in order to help break up such pathological relating and to help family members replace it with something more healthy.

Like any other form of therapy, family therapy is not always effective, but it can very often work wonders. As one mother reported to us:

> Things were so bad in our household and I became so desperate that I got up my courage and insisted that we all four see a family therapist. Both our boys in these sessions tend to be more or less their usual hostile, belligerent, quarrelsome selves, but still they *are* improving. My husband is the surprise and delight.
>
> I would never have believed that this strong, definite, aggressive, "always right" man would sit there and take part in these self-revealing sessions. I would just like to share with other mothers of teen-age boys what seems to me like a miracle. If other mothers share my problem of constant turmoil in their households, I hope they will try my solution.

Parenting Programs

In the last two decades a relatively new way of helping parents cope with the many problems of child raising has developed. This is the notion of parenting classes and workshops.

The idea is not entirely new. As long ago as the 1940's some of us turned up, week after week, to give a series of lectures to some groups of interested parents. Today's parenting classes are much more active and involve more participation by the parent-members than the earlier lecture series.

At first, parenting classes were rather general and covered many or all aspects of bringing up children. Recently, specialists have begun offering workshops on sibling relationships.

Such workshops are at a lighter and perhaps less formidable level than the more formal and extended family therapy. Many parents find that, to get out of some rut or discouragement, all they need is the rather concise help and encouragement that can be obtained from sharing problems, under the supervision of qualified leadership.

Many parents have gone from despair to moderate amusement when they discover that the horrendous difficulties that have them so stymied are more or less universal or at least widely experienced by others.

Parental tolerance varies. An amount of fighting that seems to some parents absolutely intolerable may be shrugged off as normal family living in another household. We suggest that you might wish to seek outside help

If the children's fighting really bothers you.

If the fighting seems to get worse as time goes on.

If quarreling, bickering, and arguing is really ugly.

If, as is sometimes the case, the children physically harm each other.

Chapter Eleven
Then Why Not Just One?

Why—some parents may wonder, when they are right in the thick of what is euphemistically called sibling rivalry and words or blows are flying thick and fast—does anybody have more than one child? Wouldn't parents, and children themselves, be happier if this constant bone of contention (a brother or a sister) were never present?

This thought comes particularly to mind when brothers and sisters are not only hitting each other, but watching each other like hawks and/or glaring at each other with pure hatred. Why, you may then ask, put everybody through so much?

Actually there are many good reasons, aside from sheer love of children, why many people feel it is well worthwhile to have more than one child in the family.

Children in a Family Form a Subculture All Their Own

Many parents, especially parents of large families, comment that their children constitute an extremely supportive subculture all their own. It is hard for an outsider to evaluate this fully, but it does seem reasonable that there should be a certain comfort in not being the only nonadult in the family—even when intense rivalry and scrapping exist among such subculture members.

Many parents remark, "They'd murder each other, but let anybody outside the family touch one of them and that person has had it." And even when no outside danger threatens, many children seem to enjoy plotting and planning together—either for their parents or against them.

Common sense tells us that only children do grow up to be perfectly good adults and presumably do not suffer from their "onliness." And yet it is companionable and supportive to be part of a group, sharing common interests.

Having siblings is not only companionable but can also be highly instructive. It isn't always easy to get along with playmates and schoolmates. But since most people, unfortunately, are at their very worst at home, it is here that one learns what infighting is. And, of course, what contemporaries of the opposite sex are really like. These lessons stand many people in good stead. As thirteen-year-old Teresa explained it, "At camp they say terrible things to you. Having brothers and sisters gets you sort of hardened up."

The More the Merrier

Family living, as the marriage ceremony says, is clearly for better or for worse. Though much of this book deals with family problems, most of us feel that there is more good than bad to any family's living. If marriage and home life did not yield considerable reward, people all over the world would hardly continue to rush into them. (Even the majority of those who have been divorced do marry again and often start their own second families.)

Obviously much warmth and love is to be had in a family

relationship, much generosity and concern expressed among the members. Admittedly a mother, father, and one child can enjoy family times together, but when things go well, as they often do, it does seem the more the merrier.

There are few things more touching than a Christmas morning, with each individual looking anxiously to be sure that the others *like* the gifts so carefully chosen. Or to see an eleven-year-old returning from a vacation with Grandma, with something special for Mother, Dad, and Brother and Sister, and the comment, "I can't wait to see Billy and Sue."

"I Wouldn't Want to Be an Only"

Most heartening to any parent who sometimes feels that "they fight all the time" are the many, many good things children say about really enjoying their brothers and sisters and not wanting to be an only child:

- A twelve-year-old boy: "I'd rather have brothers than not. Who wants to stay in the house alone?"
- A thirteen-year-old boy: "Fun to be part of a big family of boys."
- A thirteen-year-old boy: "Ann is definitely my sister now. We took a bicycle trip about nineteen miles long. I wasn't up to it and she just barely was. She was very nice about walking up hills when I did."
- Another thirteen-year-old boy: "Glad I have brothers and sisters."
- A thirteen-year-old girl: "I'm glad I have brothers. I'd hate to be an only child."
- A thirteen-year-old girl: "I wouldn't want to be the only child because I might get spoiled."
- A fourteen-year-old girl: "It's an advantage to have older sisters. They tell me all sorts of things I wouldn't know—what to do about boys and clothes. Fun to discuss dates with them. I sure wouldn't want to be an only child."

Fun to Fight

As we've mentioned earlier, many brothers and sisters really enjoy their fights. This is obvious from the fact that a younger and perhaps weaker child who has really gotten into trouble, once rescued, may then repeat the very action that started the whole thing in the first place. We also have children's own statements about the pleasures of fighting:

- An eleven-year-old boy: "My brothers and I fight often, for the fun of it. Just scuffling around. We do it on purpose because we enjoy it."
- A thirteen-year-old boy: "I fight with my ten-year-old sister. We enjoy it. I like it and she likes it but our parents don't like it."
- A fourteen-year-old boy: "The only reason we get along well is that Dad had a talk with us and explained that one of the reasons Mother was sick and nervous so much was because we quarreled. And he asked us not to any more. So we don't. But we certainly miss it. We used to have such a good time fighting."

Siblings Try to Help Each Other Out or "Improve" Them

Brothers and sisters in any family by no means spend all their time fighting with or trying to get each other into trouble. Quite the contrary. We know of many who go out of their way to help each other out, sometimes occasionally, sometimes systematically. One of our more verbal and more imaginative ten-year-old friends explained to us the ways in which she tried to make her seven-year-old brother into a better boy:

Well, I use trickery on my brother. You see he isn't ordinarily a very good child, so in order to make him clean up his room or do things that he ordinarily ought to do you must resort to trickery of some sort. So I have made up some fairies, and if he's good enough he can go to fairyland and get fairy presents. (I go out and make the presents and pretend they are from the fairies.)

So when I want him to do something I write to him and say, "King Nebuchadnezzer or something like that wishes you to clean up your room, and you will get two steps up the fairy ladder toward fairyland for doing so. Signed, His Majesty."

Well, it works out pretty well. Then something else I do—you know those air ventilation places? At night sometimes I tell Billy to keep an eye on it for the fairy mailman who may bring some mail. Then I shine a flashlight through there and sing songs that are appropriate to the day and time that is, and pretend it's the fairy mailman. Then I make footmarks and I go over and blow it to him through his beanshooters. And every morning he says, "I've seen the king's what-you-may-call-it and I heard him singing, too." And I can hardly refrain from laughing, but I do.

And I've gotten him so far to promise that he would join the Boy's Choir, and to promise to stay in Sunday School and not play hookey just because he doesn't like the boys. And I've made him promise to join the Cub Scouts, and to clean up his room on Saturday. And all this by the same trickery and if anybody ever spilled the beans, oh, I'd be murdered. But they're on the knife now because my sister knows and she can't keep anything to herself.

Or, a little more simply, a thirteen-year-old girl tells us:

My brother, Larry, he's seven. He's selfish but he can be fun sometimes. Lots of times I have to do things myself, as brush my teeth, to get him to do them. I make out a schedule every day of the week, night and morning, and then I check the times he brushes his teeth. He thinks it's a game if you do it with him.

A thirteen-year-old boy may say:

I have three sisters, three, seven, and eight. My best way to get them in a good mood is to promise them something like "Tomorrow we'll go to the movies, so be good girls."

Fourteen may tell you:

My little brother is coming along fine. It's a novelty to teach him to play baseball and to play around with him. He has a craving to learn.

Often any or all of these efforts go rather well, though as one mother put it of her older son, "He'd murder him [younger brother] trying to get him to do the right thing."

Others try not so much to control the behavior of siblings as to entertain them. A four-year-old boy may "read" to his little brother. A girl a bit older may tell stories to her brothers. Almost any fighting is preceded by minutes (hours?) of amicable play.

The good kinds of intersib relations are too numerous to mention but it might add to your own positive feeling about how well your children do, at least much of the time, to make lists, or keep a notebook recording kinds of situations in which your older children really are doing good, kind, friendly, or helpful things for younger siblings. (Or vice versa.)

Older Sibs Quite Often Help Out Those Younger

Not only do older sibs teach the younger ones, "improve" them, play with them nicely, entertain them, but very often, if so moved, they stand up for them against their parents. The younger ones, in return, are often said to "worship" their older brothers and sisters—"Thinks he's everything."

It is not uncommon for a teenager to urge his parents, "Oh, let her alone. She's a good kid." Or, "My brother is five. We get on fine. I take care of him for Mother, play with him, read to him." Or he may warn, "She's just a little kid, Mom. Don't bug her. I'll take care of that."

A parent may tell us "John [aged ten] just loves his six-year-old brother, who worships the ground he walks on. John can make Billy do anything. He has more influence on him than I do."

Or a girl reports, "I like taking care of her and having a sister. She minds me better than she minds Mother."

Selected Comments from the Literature on Childhood

The notion that there is great value to having brothers and sisters is not new with us. Fiction (as well as, very likely, your own life experience) abounds with examples. Here are just a handful of typical comments from some professionals and one parent.

Brian Sutton-Smith and B. G. Rosenberg (47):

> Next to the intimate nature is the stark frankness of the sibling relationship. It is not one of company manners with doting parents hovering near to smooth out tangles and irregularities. Relationships between siblings permit little or no dissembling. In the terms of the baseball world, each solves the delivery of the other early in the game. No tricks will suffice, no deceptions will work.
>
> Siblings come to know each other by the book. They come to live largely with each other—to use the vernacular again—"with their hair down." Life among siblings is like living in the nude, psychologically speaking.
>
> Siblings serve as a constant crude awakening. On the other hand, siblings save each other from being with their parents and other adults too much. The significance of this is that they are kept from the unnatural environment which the adult furnishes. Parents and other adults are less satisfactory companions for children than are other children because children treat each other more like equals. Siblings feel that they understand each other and each other's problems, and that often they do so better than the parents.

Lee Salk, in his popular book for parents (40), expresses his opinion that it is definitely to any child's advantage to have siblings, since siblings create certain stresses, which, if overcome successfully, help give the child resources that can be adapted to deal with other situations later in life. Furthermore, if a child has siblings, he sees his parents dealing with different children in different ways. Any child can learn a lot by watching his parents deal with the other children in the family.

Victor Cicirelli (12) stresses the fact that within the family, siblings may definitely influence each other to a greater extent than parents. And Donald Irish (29) points out correctly that siblings can and do fulfill a number of functions in a child's life. They act as parent substitutes, teachers of youthful skills, role models, challengers, and stimulators. It is certainly true that in many instances children learn from siblings more easily and with less resistance than they learn from parents. This can be especially true in the teenage years when both boys and girls often accept advice and suggestions from older sibs much more readily than they do from parents.

And McDermott (33) reminds us that

> A sibling relationship lasts a lifetime, longer than the parent-child relationship. In some parts of the world, it's considered the most important kinship tie, even more important than marriage or the one between parents and children. When brothers and sisters are three and four years old, they spend twice as much time together as they do with their parents. Competition between them can be a constructive experience and can strengthen a youngster for success in later life. Or it can continue on as a bitter battle toward everyone in life.

And now for a somewhat lighter-hearted comment from Teresa Bloomingdale (8), herself the mother of ten:

> If there is anything more inspiring than watching a new baby sleeping in his crib, it is watching an "old baby" watching the new baby sleeping in his crib. A two-year-old standing on tiptoe, peeking into the crib; a four-year-old on hands and knees, laughingly trying to teach the baby to creep; a six-year-old sitting beside the baby's bed thoughtfully considering the intricacies of a tiny baby's ear; an eight-year-old trying to teach his baby brother how to hold a football; a ten-year-old tenderly placing her favorite doll in his baby sister's bassinette; a twelve-year-old awkwardly and surreptitiously lifting his baby sister from her crib for a quick but loving hug . . . these are the things that make motherhood wonderful and will, I hope, explain once and for all why I had so many kids. . . .
>
> Just consider some of these joys and blessings:
> In a big family, when one child says "Anybody want to go outside and toss a football around?" he's got an instant team.

For the "little brother" in a big family, there is always a big brother to take you to camp-outs and games and scout meetings, and a big sister to iron on your scout badges and listen to your riddles and tease the tears away if Mama's not around.

On the other hand, if you are the "big brother" in a big family, there is always a little brother who can be bribed to run an errand for you, or a little sister who can be cajoled into taking your turn at the dishes.

Being a child in a big family means if you can't find your coat, it's okay; there's an extra one hanging in the closet.

Members of a big family never argue about where to go on their vacation because they never take a vacation.

The oldest child in a big family gets a lot of attention because his or her parents feel he was cheated out of his babyhood by the rapid arrival of younger siblings.

The youngest child in a big family gets a lot of attention because there are no more babies for everybody to fawn over.

The middle children in a big family get a lot of attention because they learn early in life to *demand* it.

And Then You Grow Old

And now we project far into the future—to a time when you yourselves are really quite elderly and your children themselves are grown. Admittedly it takes a good deal of foresight to imagine such a time. And certainly if you don't like children and don't want a big family, having them just so they might look out for you when you are old would be unrealistic.

In earlier times many people liked to have as many children as possible because, at least in farm communities, children were needed to help with the work. And since money was often extremely scarce, it was pretty much taken for granted that some or several of the children would look out for their aged parents when the time came for them to do so.

Society doesn't quite function that way anymore, yet still the time does come for many when they no longer can look out for themselves. Thus even if you are financially secure, you may need help from your children in planning your lives. It is if and when some arrangement has to be made (whether providing care in your own home or finding an adequate place outside your home) that your child will appreciate having a sibling to help make the decisions that must be made. Such decisions are often difficult at best, excessively difficult when one has to make them alone.

And finally comes the time, perhaps hard to conceive, when you are gone and with you, unless your child has siblings, shared memories of his childhood and of himself as a child. An only child can remember, of course, but remembering all by one's self can be a lonely matter. Giving your child siblings with whom to share his memories is a gift indeed.

Rather a far projection, admittedly, from the time when, as one mother put it, her children "quarreled as naturally as they breathed." But the time does come, and it is as much a part of one's lifelong course as those earlier times.

Brothers and sisters do eventually serve their purpose very well.

There Are Also Advantages to Parents

Children themselves are not the only ones advantaged by belonging to a multichild family. Many parents find it easier to have several children than just one. Many parents tell us, each seeming to feel that he has coined the thought, "If we could just throw away the first one and start all over with our second."

Certainly there's no question but that one learns a tremendous amount from one's first adventure in parenting. Moreover, one's confidence increases, so that one is much more comfortable and effective with second, third, and later children than with the first.

More important, perhaps, is that almost any child will get away with all he can. In a family of more than one, each boy or girl loses the opportunity of being a prima donna—a role that so many "onlys" exploit to the hilt. Each age in childhood has its own personality, as we have elaborated elsewhere (28). Behavior at any given age consists of more than just the sum of the things the child is able to do—it has its own flavor and general characteristics.

Thus we think of the two-and-a-half-year-old as a person who lives between opposite extremes: "I will, I won't" . . . "I can, I can't" . . . "I want, I don't want." He is also extremely bossy and commanding: "Do this, do that" . . . "Come here" . . . "Open the door" . . . "Turn off TV." He can, if permitted to do so, run an entire household with his directives and commands.

Three-and-a-half, by contrast, is an age of great uncertainty. Body and mind seem overwhelmed with insecurity. A quite normal child of this age may stutter and stumble, tremble and twitch, fall and fumble. Most parts of living may seem too much for him. Four, at the opposite extreme, tends to be out-of-bounds in every area of functioning—motor, adaptive, language, and personal-social. He boasts. He lies. He swears. He exaggerates. He thrives on going outside established boundaries.

An only child, at any of these remarkable ages, can dominate a household with his very special ways of behaving. But if your family consists of two or three or more of these little persons, no single one has the opportunity to act out his own scenario fully. There just isn't time and attention to spare, and thus no one child, no matter how great his demands or requirements, is able to tyrannize the family with his age-related needs. One sees glimpses of these needs, most surely and clearly, but there is just no way that they can attain that degree of predominance the only child quite easily achieves.

One further advantage to parents of having more than one child is that their worries are spread around. Most conscientious parents do worry about their children—about their toilet training, their eating, their manners and morals, their social and academic achievements. When there is only one child in the family, an abnormal amount of family anxiety tends to focus on some one simple area of failure—and that very anxiety often exaggerates the problem to an unhealthy degree. A parent has only so much worrying time and energy available. Best to spread it out over several children and several problems than to be entirely focused on one.

Chapter Twelve

Things Do Get Better

This would hardly be a Gesell book if we did not discuss the fact that behavior does change, somewhat predictably, with age. And that, in general, the change is for the better.

However, in the case of sibling relationships it must be admitted that the hoped-for change is often very slow in arriving. (It is discouraging but not unusual to see even a fourteen-year-old fighting physically with a sibling.)

So the outlook is both good and bad—good in that things almost surely will improve; bad in that improvement usually takes much longer than you might hope. And also a bit discouraging in that, until the time comes when things do improve, they tend to be rather worse than most new parents anticipate.

It is hoped that a realistic overview of what one can expect in the first sixteen years of life may help you parents to keep up your courage and your quite realistic hope that "this too shall pass."

In the following pages, the characteristic behavior of each group, year by year, is described. These observations and reports outline the long, slow, and often painful stages by which the normal boy or girl in our culture arrives at the place where at least much of the time he or she will enjoy and appreciate brothers and sisters.

Eighteen Months

The usual Eighteen Monther is so extremely self-centered that play with any other children, siblings or others, tends to be at a minimum.

As a rule he will pay only brief attention to any baby siblings. His attention is usually only very fleeting.

Older siblings as a rule, when interested, are reasonably kind and caring of this young person. For the most part he does not offer much competition, since any squabbles over toys usually end up in favor of the older child.

Some older siblings take great pleasure in "teaching" the Eighteen Monther, and because he has great imitative abilities, he may learn quite a lot from them. Thus if a brother or sister tells him, "Doug, say 'Moo,' " or "Doug, say 'Quack quack,' " or in an excess of good manners, "Say 'Thanks Mom,' " Eighteen Monthers will very likely oblige: "Moo," "Quack quack," or "Thanks Mom." This kind of imitation undoubtedly does help speed up verbalization.

In fact the child of this age tends to learn a good deal in all respects from older siblings, who if there is a reasonable distance between them in age usually treat him rather kindly.

Two-and-a-half-year-olds, who have not yet learned to share, tend to grab, push, and show little patience with Eighteen Monthers. And if two siblings this close to an age start fighting, it may be almost impossible to separate them. A jump rope can be lying idle nearby till one grabs it. Then the other suddenly wants it, too, and a real tug-of-war may ensue. Physically removing either the jump rope or the children may be your only recourse.

Two Years

Most Twos or even Two-and-a-halfs do not have vast difficulty with siblings, especially if sibs are substantially older or younger. Except in a rather crowded family, Two is likely to be the youngest of the lot. Older sibs either quite naturally treat him reasonably well, since he is the "baby," or at least are admonished by their parents that they *must* treat him well.

Older sibs are told not to hit him, not to grab his toys, and to let him play with them. If trouble ensues in spite of these admonitions, parents are usually quick to protect his rights.

With younger siblings, Twos vary. Some are extremely protective, thoughtful, friendly, and even tender. Others—if they are insecure themselves or people make too much fuss over the new baby—may be extremely hostile, jealous, and even attacking.

Sometimes rough treatment of the baby occurs simply because Two does not appreciate his own strength and the relative fragility of the infant. Sometimes it occurs intentionally because he really wishes to do harm.

If your Two seems likely to harm his baby sister or brother, a lot of talk to the effect that "We must treat Baby nicely" won't do much good. The pair will need to be watched and kept apart. A Two could, only partly unintentionally, do considerable harm to an unwatched baby.

Most Twos find life with others relatively easy. Two-and-a-halfs have the problem of wanting solid possession of any toy they have been playing with, are playing with, or might play with. Thus Two-and-a-half may sit in his wagon, with the wagon and his arms full of toys, feet protecting toys he cannot encompass with hands and arms. Or his feet may extend to protect other toys, which he has ranged beside his wagon. If a sibling touches any object in the room, Two-and-a-half is likely to call out "Mine!"

This possessiveness gives most trouble with siblings very close to him in age. Younger or just slightly older sibs may or may not accept deprivation (their toy being grabbed away from them) calmly. It helps if Mother is nearby to provide a substitute. Much older sibs can usually hold their own, though considerable pulling, tugging, yelling, and hitting are likely to take place.

Most trouble occurs, especially around Two-and-a-half, if siblings are very close in age. A Two-and-a-half, if sandwiched in between a Fifteen Monther and a Three-and-a-half or Four, may seem to be in almost constant difficulty—either beating up his younger sib or getting beaten up by the older. Even a basically sweet-tempered child may be in difficulty during much of the day. Keeping her children separated (or closely supervised) may be a mother's best defense.

Cooperative, sharing play is beyond most Twos or even Two-and-a-halfs.

Three Years

The extent to which the Three-year-old gets on with siblings depends very definitely on the family constellation. This is always true, of course, but possibly more so now than at other ages. If all brothers and sisters are substantially older than he, chances are things will go rather well. Three, by nature, is a somewhat peaceable little soul. Older sibs tend to find him amusing and likable. And if he is grabby, or given to tantrums, they are often quite willing to smooth things over.

As to younger, or just-older sibs, behavior varies from one day to the next, even from hour to hour. Three, and even more so Three-and-a-half, tends to be highly unpredictable. He can be protective and friendly to a younger sibling on one occasion, even under considerable provocation, and on another may straight-arm the baby on even the slightest provocation.

Since the Three-and-a-half tends to be full of "Don't look"'s,

"Don't talk"'s, "Don't laugh"'s, any sibling of any age is likely, quite unwittingly, to break his rules. Then trouble ensues.

Three probably has the most difficulty with Two and Four. Just-younger sibs tend to be grabby; just-older, pushy and wild and very impatient. Thus if Three is blessed with one or more siblings close to him in age, any moment of any day may be a moment of fuss and turmoil. As parents often comment, if you take your eyes off them for a minute, they can be in trouble. All too many, either intentionally or unintentionally, do physical harm to each other. The most loving and ingenious mother in the world cannot possibly foresee or prevent all trouble. Family rules of "We don't hit," "We don't kick," fall on deaf ears. Some marvel that preschoolers in a closely spaced family survive.

Three's reaction to a baby sib depends largely on his own individuality. A very secure Three may be extremely gentle, kind, and friendly to the new arrival. One who has been favored and pampered, and who himself may not feel particularly secure, may look on the new arrival with marked disfavor, may make adverse comments, suggest that you take the baby back, or may even harm him physically. Reasonable tact and an extremely watchful eye should be enough to avoid major confrontation.

Four Years

We have described the typical Four-year-old as wild, wonderful, and out-of-bounds. Nowhere may he be more out-of-bounds than in his relationships with siblings.

This doesn't mean that Four may not on occasion be thoughtful and kind to a baby sibling. And he may follow an older sib, especially a brother, like a little puppy dog.

Four is usually old enough that, unless he is having real emotional problems in growing up and in being superseded by somebody younger, he will much of the time be reasonably good to a baby sibling. But even now he should not be trusted alone with a baby, at least not for any long period of time. Even those who are normally quite good with those much younger, may be suddenly quite mean to a baby. Like the boy who, quite unprovoked, said to his baby sister, all dressed up in a new pink dress, "Pink, pink, you stink!"

Relations with sibs between Three and Six are often stormy indeed. Four, in his exaggerated way, comes down very hard on both brothers and sisters—verbally and, if they are smaller, physically.

"Dat's not the way to do it," he may say to a six-year-old sib. "If you do dat once more, I'll cut you up into pieces and throw you in the garbage."

In addition to being out-of-bounds, Four is often extremely unpredictable. Thus he may play very nicely with a sibling of any age, but he may at times be extremely quarrelsome and rambunctious, even with those considerably older than he. Parents usually know how to handle an out-of-bounds Four, may even find his exaggerations somewhat amusing. Not so with siblings, who tend to be annoyed at the foolishness, exaggeration, lying, and profanity that often characterize Four's behavior.

It is often surprising to parents that Four can get into real trouble with a brother or sister much older. For their own reasons, sometimes unfathomed, Fours occasionally become extremely aggressive and directive toward much older siblings. Perhaps their own sense of superiority is threatened by greater competence.

Fours, both boys and girls, often get along much better with contemporaries in the supervised atmosphere of a nursery school than they do with their own siblings at home.

Five Years

Five, with siblings as with other people, tends to be in a rather good state of equilibrium. He is less bossy and less demanding than he was at Four or will be at Six, less wild than he may be at either of these surrounding ages.

As a rule he is especially good with much younger siblings, especially with any siblings under Three. He is especially kind and mothering with any infant sib—though here parents must be careful not to give Five too much responsibility and freedom. The child of this age loves to hold a baby sibling and may be allowed to do so, but only under supervision.

He is not as out-of-bounds as he was a year earlier, not as selfish and exacting as he will be in the year to come.

Five is very much better than earlier at sharing and taking turns.

However, with his wish for adult approval, the child of this age may be extremely good with younger siblings when adults are present, but may take things from them or tease them when he is with them alone.

Five tends to respond to older siblings as he does to adults. He wants to please and to do what is required of him. Thus he may be very good at taking the baby role when they are playing house, may run errands when requested.

Five may be said to "adore" a baby sibling.

However, Five has moments of jealousy if a younger sibling is receiving too much attention, and is capable of blaming some of his own acts on a younger sib.

In general, play outdoors tends to go more smoothly than play indoors, where ownership of possessions may very likely come into dispute.

Six Years

Six has trouble with nearly all siblings, both older and younger, a great deal of the time. The difficulty stems from the basic nature of his personality. Six tends to be self-centered, bossy, domineering, and grabby. He finds it difficult to take a back seat, to cooperate, to conform, to give in. In short, he lacks the basic ingredients needed to get along with other people.

Six may be less tolerant with younger siblings than he may have been earlier. He may enjoy teaching them things but may also egg them on to do "bad" things, since he likes to see them scolded and punished.

With siblings near his own age, he argues, teases, bullies, frightens, torments, fights, enjoys making them cry in any way he can.

One of Six's least endearing characteristics, for siblings, is his love of tattling. Needless to say he tattles when brother or sister hurt or bother him. But he also likes to tattle about things that have nothing to do with him, with the sole intent of getting others into trouble.

Since Six finds it totally intolerable to lose at any competitive activity, he will cheat in order to win—and then may accuse his sib of cheating.

Six tends to have a real chip on his shoulder much of the time, and this holds for siblings as well as for others.

All of this doesn't mean that quarreling is continual. Some mothers even report, "Pretty good with his brother except for the usual spats." And things tend to go better out of doors than indoors.

This is a high point for children's customary fear that things will not be even—that somebody else will be first, will have more, will get the biggest piece. This leads to much eagle-eyed monitoring of any and all situations. A child's whole day may be spoiled if a younger sibling gets to the table before he does.

Most Sixes get on very badly with older as well as with younger siblings. The Six-year-old's behavior tends to be extremely irritating to older sibs and often causes much conflict. Older siblings are not as patient with Sixes as they may be with younger sibs of other ages. "That spoiled brat," "a pest," "a nuisance," "impossible" are not unusual epithets.

Possibly Eleven-year-olds (another difficult age) and Six-year-olds make the very worst combinations, though Twelves, Thirteens, and Fourteens all have a good deal of criticism for Six. And actually Six can be a "pain in the neck" to any older siblings.

Seven Years

Seven has one characteristic that helps him get along better with siblings than was the case just a year earlier. Seven functions in a somewhat minor key, and when things go wrong for the child, as they often do, he is quite as likely to withdraw as to stay and fight it out.

Also, girl or boy is less aggressive, less competitive, than a year earlier. He tends to take a rather gloomy view of life, but complaints may be about life in general rather than about a particular sibling.

Seven thinks that people don't like him, that they treat him meanly and unfairly, and this feeling can on occasion be focused on some special sib. In such cases he will watch that sibling like a hawk and will complain about any infringement of his own "rights."

In fact this is one of the high points for complaints that things aren't "fair," that the child is not getting his equal share of whatever it is that is being distributed.

Seven tends to be somewhat less of a tattler than he was just one year earlier. Certainly he will go whining to his mother if he feels that he has been treated unfairly. But he is somewhat less likely than Six to tattle simply in order to get a sibling into difficulty.

Seven's characteristic forgetfulness sometimes causes him to forget a grudge before he gets around to getting even with a sibling.

Boy or girl now feels grown-up enough to take on the role of big brother (or big sister) to family members younger than himself. He likes to teach them and likes to protect them. If the younger sibling is a baby, he may want to carry her, feed her her bottle, or wheel her in her carriage.

However, all is not perfection. Boy or girl will at times tease, poke, bicker, and fight with younger siblings. And seven especially worries that a younger brother or sister may put something over on him or get more privileges than he.

Seven tends to admire older siblings and may even be strongly under their influence. He tends to be proud of them and to boast about them.

However, his unevenness and variability is expressed by parents with such phrases as "Bickers with sister but thinks she's cute," "Protects his sister but teases her."

A few are consistently bad, especially with those near to their own age: "They fight like cats and dogs."

Some at Seven, if they have been sharing a room with a sibling up till now, suddenly express a wish to have a room of their own.

Eight Years

The typical Eight is usually much more outgoing and aggressive than he was a year earlier. He also has a frequent chip on the shoulder and is overaware of slights or imagined insults.

Thus by his very nature, he tends to get into much difficulty with those around him, especially with his siblings. Some Eights are reported to be consistently bad with sibs—teasing, being selfish, quarreling.

Eight, with his basically outgoing nature, finds it hard to stay out of relation with any part of the environment, including siblings. And since the behavior of other people seldom comes up to his expectations, much friction ensues.

Eight tends to dramatize. Thus squabbles with siblings, as he reports them to his parents, tend to be vastly exaggerated.

Eight loves to argue and also is extremely aware of other people's mistakes. This makes him tiresome to older siblings.

At this age, boy or girl definitely does not want younger siblings tagging along, and his company is not too often welcomed by older sibs.

Some areas of behavior do show improvement. The child now can take part in competitive games and can often lose without going all to pieces as earlier.

With his antenna out to be sure that he gets his fair share, he is often extremely jealous . . . wants all privileges that any other siblings (even those considerably older) have . . . fears that sibs may put something over on him.

As at other ages, the quality of the relationship does depend to a marked extent on the ages of the siblings. With siblings Five and under, Eight may much of the time be reasonably patient and tolerant.

Siblings between Six and Ten may be too close to his own age to permit harmony. Eight all too easily gets down to the level of the younger ones. He may have lost the "big brother" attitude that he practiced at Seven, and may quickly get involved in teasing and fighting.

Eight-year-olds get on badly, as a rule, with Eleven-year-olds, who get on badly with almost everyone. They even have difficulty with Twelves, who get on well with siblings of most other ages.

But they tend to get on reasonably well with any siblings over twelve, who tend either to be relatively patient with them or to ignore them.

Nine Years

At this quieter, more thoughtful age, many children get on much better with their siblings than they did at Eight. They may be nicely protective of younger (and proud of older) sibs. There will inevitably be some difficulty if brothers or sisters are near their own age.

Nine in general, in his quiet, thoughtful way, may actually be quite good with much younger siblings if he is made responsible for them. He can in such circumstances often be extremely understanding, without the strictness and sternness he may have exhibited a year earlier.

Inevitably there may be considerable difficulty with siblings close in age. He may argue, fight verbally or physically, compete, accuse.

Friends are extremely important to the typical Nine. As will be the case increasingly later on, girl or boy may have somewhat less time for siblings and thus may get into a little less trouble than earlier.

In the presence of contemporaries, Nine may be much embarrassed or disgusted by the behavior of siblings and may feel that his parents should make them behave better than they do.

Nine is a strong age for interest in fairness. The child of this age may want to be sure that everything (blame included) is distributed fairly and so may be unduly upset if he feels he is being blamed for something not his fault. He is especially interested in "who started it."

Nine may on occasion show real loyalty to a sib who may be in trouble, standing up for that sib when the occasion demands.

Nine may play quite nicely with a sibling of Ten much of the time, but fighting and bickering are common, wrestling if the two are boys, and much name calling in any event.

Many have trouble with Elevens, since Elevens have trouble with almost anybody. And even at Twelve the older is often much bugged and bothered by the mere existence of a Nine-year-old sibling. "He [the Nine] hits me but I'm not allowed to hit him" is a common complaint.

With a sib of Thirteen or older, Nine gets on much better. Thirteen and Nine are in general somewhat quiet, withdrawn ages, and this may be one reason for this improvement in harmony. They just leave each other alone.

However, with sibs of Fourteen, things may take a turn for the worse. The older sib may complain that Nine bothers him, annoys him, gets into his things. Discord now may amount more to general criticism of Nine than to any excessive amount of squabbling or fighting.

If Nine's older sibs are Fifteen or Sixteen, regardless of how bad things may have been earlier, a parent may reasonably hope for a marked improvement—even a "very nice" relationship between the two.

Ten Years

The majority of Tens fight with their brothers and sisters—at least younger ones (except infants), at least part of the time. In typically balanced Ten fashion, boy or girl summarizes: "Sometimes I get on with them and sometimes I don't." Or, "He's always teasing me but I'm glad I have a brother."

A minority express strong antagonism: "That spoiled brat! Sometimes I feel as if I hated the sight of her" . . . "I'd like to smash her face in!" Whether or not rivalry and jealousy are real seems to depend more on individuality and special situation than on age.

Fighting is most frequent with younger siblings. The usual pattern is that the younger one teases, needles, taunts, or pesters until Ten finally retaliates physically. Then the younger one calls for help, or a parent steps in spontaneously. Then Ten thinks parent is unfair. Most still feel that younger siblings are favored, and also that they "get away with a lot of stuff I never got away with."

With younger siblings close to Ten's own age, though there is much good-natured playing together, fighting and bickering are very common. Fighting involves name calling ("Pig," "Fatty," "Dope"), "wrassling," and fighting intended to hurt—pushing, kicking, hitting, biting. Good-natured "wrassling" becomes real fighting when someone is hurt. Much fighting over possessions: "We both want the same thing."

Some Tens know they are not good to younger siblings: "If I want to play with him, I'm nice, but if I want to be alone, he's a *goner!*" Younger ones are often reported to "adore" Ten, but some feel that Tens are too bossy and try too hard to keep them in line.

Ten often tries to improve younger siblings and make them mind. Some mothers say "She has more influence on him than we do." Efforts to make younger siblings behave range from simple admonition to elaborate and inventive scheming.

Tens get on better with older than with younger siblings, and report that older ones sometimes play with them or take them places, though there is still a lot of fighting. Many know that older siblings consider them a nuisance or tattletale because they sometimes seek protection from parents.

Certainly there is improvement in sibling relationships at this age. Parents report, "They get on better than they used to."

Eleven Years

Elevens tend to have trouble with their brothers and sisters as with everybody else. In fact, many are worse with sibs at Eleven than they were a year earlier. They seem by nature quarrelsome and difficult. They find it hard to live and let live, have a big chip on their shoulders.

Like Ten, Eleven tends to be rather ambivalent in the evaluation of siblings: "Well, once in a while I think I'll never get along without him and other times I think, 'Oh, if he was only away!' Sometimes I really blow up and start kicking him. We certainly do have fun together, though."

Elevens in general get on badly much of the time with younger siblings (except the very young). Fighting varies from "occasionally" to "about half the time." And though physical fighting is giving way to verbal argument and name calling, violence still occurs—hitting, biting, pulling hair, scratching.

Much "needling" occurs, both physical and verbal: "She can't go by without touching him—just a little poke or jab. Then he reciprocates. Then a real physical battle."

All too often the younger siblings do get away with things that Eleven can't get away with, and this causes resentment. "My brother goes 'Waah' and jumps into my parents' arms. I can't do that. I'm too old. And if I do, he will say, 'Oh, look at the little crybaby.' But if we're outside, and I can do what I want, I grab him by the hair and feel I would like to rip out all his hair by the roots and tear him to pieces, I get so mad." Or, "Richie can yell and do anything he wants to at the table, but if I touch the table leg with my foot, I'm sent upstairs to bed."

As at Ten, an older child resents it that a younger sib needles him, and then when he retaliates, parents tend to blame him. "My little sister gets me into trouble on purpose. 'Nya, nya, Petie, can't catch me.' Then she runs to play tag but Mother doesn't allow me to play tag in the house. If she starts it, Mother doesn't do anything, but if I start it, Mother blames me and punishes me."

Eleven is very critical of faults of younger siblings—thinks they are lazy, messy, careless, untruthful. Often yells at younger siblings though complains that older siblings yell at him.

Possessions cause much difficulty: "He gets into my things." However, Elevens are beginning to develop their own techniques for solving such problems. Some lock the door to keep out very young siblings, "try to ignore" ones nearer their own age.

Feel that younger ones tag along too much, though sometimes they play nicely with them and are even glad of their company. "Glad to have him. I like to have someone to hang around with me. He bothers my things a little but not much."

Eleven tries to correct and boss younger sibs. Often this is resented. But some use good techniques and may report, "She minds me better than she does Mother." May help with younger sibs in a quite grown-up way, though this may deteriorate into squabbles: "When I undress him at night, he sometimes runs out of the room and says, 'You can't hurt me.' But sometimes I catch him and hit him and sit on him. I consider it my privilege because I'm the boss in my own room."

Conversely, Elevens object when older siblings try to boss them.

Almost every sib feels that it is important to have the last word. Or two may fight about the principle of things rather than over actual material possessions: "It wasn't the book. It was the principle of the thing. If I don't win this time, I'll never win again. I just can't lose this time."

Most Elevens get on reasonably well with most siblings who are considerably older than they. But they may say of those just a few years older, "We fight some but not as much as we did." Fighting with older siblings may now be more verbal than physical: "We don't hit each other, just argue."

Eleven worries that his brothers and sisters prefer each other to him, or gang up against him.

A big advance is the beginning of appreciation that some or much of the time parents *are* fair, and even that parents see their point of view: "Tommy is seven. I tease him and hit him some but we get on pretty well . . . When there's trouble, my parents will hear my side of the story" . . . "He minds me fairly well if I don't yell at him but sometimes I get mad and yell. I think my parents know it's his fault at his age, and they don't blame me too much" . . . "My brother is three. He's pretty good most of the time but he likes to bother people. When he gets to the point of breaking things, I just pick him up *very gently* and put him out the door and close the door in his face. Then he cries and kicks the door. Then my mother comes and says 'Come downstairs, dear,' *because she knows I wouldn't have thrown him out if he hadn't been doing something wrong.*"

However, the "not fair" aspect still looms large in the minds of many: "It's not fair that I get punished when he started it" . . . "It's not fair that he can get away with it, and I can't."

A significant comment by one Eleven: "We never quarrel when Daddy is home, because he doesn't like it."

Twelve Years

Relationships tend to improve with increasing age between siblings. Many Twelves are very good with brothers and sisters Five or under. Also good with brothers and sisters Fifteen or Sixteen and over: "Idolizes her" . . . "Admires him."

Most are very good with younger sibs: "I take care of him for Mother" . . . "We get on fine" . . . "I play with him and read to him" . . . "I like him. He's fun." May even change diapers and dress a younger sib.

The most difficulty comes with Eights and Nines. These tease and taunt him, bother him, hang around too much, pester him to play games, get into his things. "He hits me but I'm not allowed to hit him" is a common complaint. "He gets away with things I never got away with" . . . "She tells lies" . . . "He's a tattle tale."

Twelve expresses a great lack of enthusiasm for those just younger: "Oh, I guess he's all right" . . . "Guess I have to say I like having a sister" . . . "She's terrible!" The amount of fighting ranges from occasional quarrels to "always fighting," or "Once in a while we have a break and don't fight. On the average we fight once a day, sometimes more."

Nor are things too good with sibs of Thirteen and Fourteen: "We're always fighting—sometimes with words, sometimes with fists."

There are encouraging signs of trying to *understand* their siblings. May say of those younger, "If he's real mad, I just go to my room and shut my door" . . . "When I get mad, I hit him but I'm trying to control myself." Or Twelve may say, smiling tolerantly, "He gets away with a lot."

And of those older he may say, "He teases me but only in fun and I tease him right back. He never beats me up or hurts me" . . . "She does yell at me but it's mostly my fault" . . . "I realize she's just teasing me and doesn't really dislike me."

Many now seem to feel that parents side with them in case of difficulty: "They take my side if there is a quarrel" . . . "She tells lies so they believe me" . . . "My mother says he's just going through a stage."

In families of more than two children, Twelve appreciates that often two can get on well together but that more than two make difficulty: "Just too many" . . . "It's just too complicated."

The majority, no matter how much they quarrel, say they are glad they have siblings: "Wouldn't want to be the only one."

Thirteen Years

Most Thirteens get on quite well with older and much younger siblings, sometimes expressing real affection for the latter. Most still have trouble with those just a few years younger, but this trouble is usually less constant than earlier and often is just general trouble. Instead of listing specific complaints, as earlier, they may say, "Don't know exactly what it's about." Fighting may also be less bitter. Real hatred for a younger sibling is rare but happens occasionally. Younger siblings, however, may like or even "adore" this same older brother or sister who "hates" them.

Many who say they still fight, especially with those just below them in age, admit to enjoying it: "Fight with my ten-year-old sister. We enjoy it, but my parents don't like it."

Many say, "We get on much better than we did." Several pinpoint the time of improvement as "Started improving about two years ago."

Worst difficulty seems to be with Ten and Eleven, with whom some "argue and fight all the time," and with Six and Seven, whom they describe as "a pest," "a nuisance," "awful," "impossible," "spoiled brat." Thirteen is critical of younger sibs: They lie, are messy, ask stupid questions.

Many quarrels, especially with those younger, are still about the younger ones getting into their things, "bothering me," "tagging along." But some objections are to personality characteristics: "He's spoiled" . . . "She's selfish."

Fighting is now more verbal than physical though some physical fighting still occurs. Occasionally Thirteen says very mean things to or about younger siblings: "Who could like that stupid so-and-so?" . . . "She's just a queer." Then these younger ones talk back: "Mind your own business." Or they mimic and mock.

Many Thirteens just try to boss younger sibs, but some are mature enough to use techniques: "I make out a schedule every day of the week, night and morning. Check times when he brushes his teeth. He thinks it's a game if I do it with him."

Also, may admit that he himself used to do things he objects to in younger sibs: "She bothers me. Gets into my things and asks stupid questions like, 'How many more miles?' Of course I used to do it too, but it *is* annoying."

Some, however, are very vindictive in dealing with younger sibs: "He's going to improve or he's going to be the sorriest kid around here. I'll club him till he does what I tell him to. It may not work, but it will give me satisfaction."

Some Thirteens, with their moody ways and passion for privacy, are touchier with siblings than they may have been at Twelve.

In some families, Thirteens are punished for mistreating younger siblings, as by deductions from their allowances. But parents often side with Thirteen a little more, recognizing faults of the younger children. This helps out.

Insight into relationships with siblings is increasing: "Probably partly my fault. He wouldn't pester me if he didn't get any reaction." "Later she won't find it so attractive to bother me, but right now I'm sort of touchy." Or, with some humor, "We get on fairly well. For instance, when he's asleep."

The majority, even when complaining, spontaneously say they are glad that they have brothers and/or sisters: "Glad I have them. If I didn't, the kids at school would think I was spoiled" . . . "Very convenient. I can tell her things and she understands" . . . "At camp they say terrible things to you. Your brothers and sisters get you sort of hardened up" . . . "Glad I have brothers. I wouldn't want to be an only child" . . . "Wish I had a brother but wouldn't swap one of my sisters for a brother."

A marked improvement occurs in relations with older siblings, even those close to Thirteen in age. Not only may they not fight but may even express positive affection: "She's definitely my sister now" . . . "We're the best of friends" . . . "Fine to be part of a big family of boys. We pal around together. Go on double dates."

Thirteen is described by parents as "devoted" to older siblings, admiring, proud, boasts about them, "thrilled with a word of praise." May admit "I know I get more privileges than he used to have."

Quarreling with other siblings is now only occasional among most Thirteens. May evaluate response of older sib and behave accordingly: "One of my brothers can't stand being teased, so I tease him. Other one doesn't tease much and doesn't mind being teased so I don't tease him."

An occasional real personality clash between Thirteen and some siblings continues from earlier times.

In general, parents are somewhat encouraged by Thirteen's improving relationship with siblings, but far from entirely satisfied.

Fourteen Years

In his relations with siblings, Fourteen usually shows some improvement over years past but still leaves much to be desired (by parents), especially in his relations with those closest to him in age. Most trouble is with Elevens. However, several Fourteens say that they actually get on better with sibs than parents realize.

With very young siblings—Five or under—most Fourteens get on very well. Take care of them, play with them, protect them, think they are "cute," even buy them things. May "push them around in a pleasant way."

The trouble occurs with those between Six and Thirteen. Fourteen has many complaints about them, specifically that they "bother" him, or "annoy" him, get into his things, tag him around. "She acts sassy and pouts if she doesn't get her own way" . . . "She laughs when I'm trying to read" . . . "I find it hard to concentrate when she's around" . . . "I get mad at her but I really think she's a great kid." Several do say, in self-criticism, that they "should" treat younger siblings better than they do. Or say "I can manage him but I have to work around him."

Fourteen's complaints also include criticism of younger sibling's behavior or personality: "Shows off all the time" . . . "Wants to be the center of attention" . . . "Makes noises and moves around so" . . . "When she isn't talking, she's singing or dancing" . . . "Wants me to do everything for her but doesn't want to do a thing for me" . . . "I hate the way she talks baby talk."

Marked individual differences in Fourteen's relations with older siblings. Mostly get on rather well—go to dances or sports events together. Older siblings give them advice: "My sister tells me all sorts of things that I wouldn't know about boys and clothes" . . . "Brothers tell you what's wrong with you and help you get dates." Considerable hero worship of older sibs.

However, Fourteens often criticize the way older siblings treat the family: "He's rude and unappreciative." Or object to siblings' "attitudes" about things. Or may think older sib doesn't treat his friends nicely. And Fourteen may be self-conscious about older sibling's criticism: "I'm always conscious of myself when she's around. If it's my friends and I want to impress them, I'm conscious of her being there.''

Many do appreciate the chance to teach younger siblings: ''He's coming along fine. It's a novelty to teach him to play baseball'' . . . ''He likes to watch me do things and I let him.''

Most, if they comment at all, say they would *not* want to be an only child. Some like the sex of sibs they have: ''I like having sisters. No sense having a brother—just competition.'' Others would prefer the opposite sex to what they have: ''I'd rather someone would be leaving a football in my room than a doll'' . . . ''A boy would be craving to learn [to play ball].''

Except with those much older, and in spite of difficulties, most say they do ''play together'' with siblings quite often, especially if none of their friends is available. Many admit, ''We have quite a lot of fun together.''

Fourteen may recognize and comment that if one member of a family is out of sorts, it spoils things for everyone. Some admit to less than perfect behavior on their own part.

Though most disagreements are verbal, some are physical: ''I get mad and hit him'' . . . ''Slug him whenever I get the chance.'' Verbal attack can be cruel: ''You're just a fat so-and-so.'' And Mother may say, ''Meals are a nightmare.'' Considerable making fun of younger sibs. However for some, telling what's wrong with younger siblings may now be offered as helpful criticism and not as hostility.

Though parents do need to step in to protect the younger children from Fourteen, the boy or girl at this age, conversely, sometimes steps in to protect younger sibs from their parents: ''Won't let us criticize her sister.''

Many seem quite satisfied with parents' impartiality.

Fifteen Years

Relations with younger siblings are definitely improving. Particularly do Fifteens get on well with much younger siblings, who look up to, imitate, and boast about them. They admit they enjoy this admiration. Some help with the younger ones, as by taking over their bedtimes. Often Fifteen will not allow parents to criticize them: "She's a good kid; let her alone." Most are exceptionally fond of and good with infants. (Though one boy says, "The baby is kinda noisy. I just don't pay any attention. The dog is really smarter.")

Fifteen's chief complaints are that the younger ones are spoiled; they do not mind parents well, do not mind him: "He just plain won't mind and then I blow my top." Other complaints are that the young ones annoy Fifteen ("Making so much noise when I'm practicing"), and tease to play with him. Some fifteens are now willing, and able, to use effective techniques with the younger ones.

With brothers and sisters near their own age, Fifteens often become very companionable: "We hack around together a lot" . . . "We have more interests in common now—a real change." Some arguing and fighting still occurs, but some say, "We always get caught when we're disagreeing, so I think our parents think we get on worse than we really do."

Some seem to feel that siblings are improving: "She's a lot cuter than she was" . . . "More intelligent than she used to be" . . . "Used to be a nuisance but not now."

Relationships with older siblings generally range from good to excellent. At worst, Fifteen says, "We get along okay. Don't see too much of each other." Moderate enthusiasm is more often expressed: "Now we're getting older we pal around more. We fight a little but not much." Many express the greatest enthusiasm: "Real good friends. Very close. We talk things over." Parents report, "He idolizes his older brother."

A few still squabble or fight occasionally. But many can now ignore a troublesome sibling, or can walk away from trouble. And several even report, "Haven't had a fight for months. We just marked our last fight and decided not to fight anymore."

Sixteen Years

By Sixteen, most get on well with older and much younger siblings, and at least don't have much trouble with those just younger. Most report marked improvement, and many attribute this to their own increased age. Some can even criticize and thus improve on their own behavior toward siblings: "I was too bossy with him."

The improvement is also probably due to the fact that Sixteens see less of siblings than they did and that their friends are now much more important to them. Sixteen enjoys the admiration of younger siblings and may like to consult older ones, but generally spends little time with either.

A few are still jealous that parents favor and "spoil" younger ones. And some teasing of and by Sixteens goes on—much enjoyed by the one who does the teasing.

But in general, most Sixteens are less involved with brothers and sisters just as they are less involved with parents, than earlier. Their thoughts and emotions tend to be focused on their own friends, of both sexes, and on themselves. It is now much less exciting to tangle with siblings.

Special Suggestions

To cover all of this ground thoroughly, one would need to write out a separate prescription for every possible combination of two ages, for every individual child, and quite likely for every day in the week. Even the most predictable individuals tend to be unpredictable in relation to their siblings.

However, here are a few possibilities:

Since the normal Two-and-a-half tends to want, need, and claim any toy that he has played with, is playing with, or might play with, a wise parent acts accordingly. She does not waste time and effort in talking to him about sharing.

Rather she will explain his grabbiness to older siblings and arrange for them to play elsewhere. Since any sib younger than a Two-and-a-half tends to be relatively pliable, she will try to arrange that he play in a separate part of the playroom, and if even then tangles arise, she will try to be available to see that the younger child at least has something in his hands. Even the grabbiest Two-and-a-half doesn't have the physical capacity to comandeer every single toy in the household.

Sixes and their siblings have difficulty not so much over things as they do over competition. Most Sixes find it extremely difficult if not impossible to lose in any competitive game with good grace and without tears. Thus a wise parent will arrange that her Six play competitive board games (the source of the greatest difficulties) either with younger sibs whom they can easily beat, or with older sibs (or adults) who will occasionally, with grace, allow themselves to be beaten.

Some of the most bitter squabbles among siblings involve each child's possessions. Brothers and sisters tend to get into or "bother" a child's "things." Often very strong parental measures are required to protect each child's treasures. At older ages, and when children are lucky enough to have their own rooms, each child's room can be out-of-bounds for siblings. Or some parents go so far as to permit locks on doors. If sibs share a room, some will actually accept a line (real or imaginary) drawn down the middle of the room, each child having his own side.

More difficult—in fact basically impossible unless one has a tremendous sense of humor, vast ingenuity, and incredible patience—is the problem presented when one child touches or looks at something belonging to another.

Rex Polier, in an article in the *Saturday Review* under the heading "Your Move, Dr. Ilg," reports that

> I have just completed several complicated hours trying to sift the causes of disputes among my young. *Real* disputes, the sort that child psychologists out of sheer cowardice or cussedness never grapple with in their books or newspaper columns. For example:

1. Emily, age seven, claims sister Mary, age nine, *touched* her bed. Emily admits that she, in retaliation, then *touched* Mary's bed and that Mary struck her.
2. Mary's version is that Emily started it by *touching* her on her left foot.
3. Enter John, age five. He accuses both girls of entering his room without his permission and looking at his goldfish.

Almost any older child's major complaint about siblings may be that they not only get into his "things," but that they hang around, tag along, bother him when he is playing with his friends. A certain amount of putting up with the company of younger sibs can fairly be required of any boy or girl. But it is up to parents to see to it that this demand is not excessive. How much is too much will vary from family to family, but any child should be permitted a reasonable amount of time out of the presence of younger sibs.

Postscript

And so it goes: "He hit me first" . . . "You like her better than me" . . . "I always get the worst of it" . . . "It isn't *fair!*"

One of the most creative bits of parenting that any individual can accomplish is to help his children get on with each other. This will be easier to accomplish in some families than in others, and there is no foolproof method that we or any others can recommend.

Clearly we cannot tell you how to keep things always smooth in your household. We cannot tell you how to prevent all squabbling, or even exactly what to do when it occurs.

But we can tell you, in the words of Dr. Arnold Gesell, that the likelihood is very good that your children are no worse than anybody else's.

We can tell you that this, too, will pass.

We can tell you that it is definitely possible to find out why at least some of the quarreling that bugs you so occurs. And with this knowledge you will be in a good position to reduce the causes and thus limit the occurrence.

We can assure you that the more you know about child behavior in general the more fully you will be able to appreciate that your own children's behavior is not unusual. Your own calm, if you believe this, will go a long way toward helping things go well in your own household. It is hoped that this book may help you to attain and to maintain that calm.

Tables

Table 1   *Source: Straus (45)*

Family Violence

Annual incidence rates per hundred couples, parents, or children, based on a nationally representative sample of 2,143 families

Type of Violence	Overall Violence Index*	Severe Violence Index†
Between spouses	16.0	6.1
Parent-to-child	63.5	14.2
Child-to-parent	18.0	9.4
Child-to-child	79.9	53.2

*Based on the occurrence of any of the following: throwing something at the other person, pushing, grabbing, shoving, slapping, kicking, biting, punching, hitting with an object, beating up, threatening to use a knife or gun, using a knife or gun.

†The same list, but excluding throwing things, pushing, grabbing, shoving, and slapping.

Table 2 *Adapted from Sutton-Smith (47)*

This Is How I Get My Sibling to Do What I Want Him to Do
(95 Fifth and Sixth Grade Students) 1–5 Point Scale from "Never" to "Always"

	Sibling Combination*							
	M1M	M1F	MM2	FM2	F1F	F1M	FF2	MF2
Violent Actions								
Beat up, belt, hit	3.00	1.80	3.06	2.50	2.44	2.33	2.67	2.22
Scratch, pinch, pull hair, bite	1.45	1.00	1.56	3.20	2.00	2.17	2.81	1.73
Tickle	2.62	2.40	2.25	3.20	3.00	3.67	3.05	2.60
Wrestle, chase	3.31	3.60	2.25	2.70	2.89	2.67	3.10	1.86
Attack things (hide toys, spoil bed)	2.38	2.20	2.31	2.50	2.67	2.00	2.38	1.80
Break things (toy, let air out of tires)	1.85	1.60	1.75	2.10	1.22	1.00	1.24	1.13
Threaten to hurt	2.92	1.80	2.13	2.70	2.44	1.67	2.33	1.80
Stop him from using phone, toys, etc.	1.62	1.80	1.19	1.90	2.33	1.50	2.71	2.08
Lock out of room	2.62	1.80	1.94	2.40	2.67	2.50	2.52	2.07
Verbal Efforts								
Promise	3.31	3.20	3.12	2.50	3.33	2.83	3.19	2.47
Boss (say "Do it," "Shut up")	3.46	3.20	2.19	3.00	3.22	4.00	2.80	2.13
Bribe, blackmail	3.23	2.60	3.44	3.60	3.56	2.33	2.52	2.60
Ask, request	3.31	2.60	3.25	3.90	3.00	3.00	2.57	2.80
Flatter	1.62	1.00	2.00	1.20	2.33	1.67	2.48	2.00
Bargain	3.54	1.80	3.19	2.00	2.67	2.83	2.95	2.33
Tell tales	1.92	1.20	2.13	1.50	1.32	1.83	2.95	1.47
Explain, persuade	3.46	2.80	3.12	2.90	2.89	3.17	3.14	2.73
Ask for sympathy	2.31	2.40	2.44	1.70	1.56	2.00	1.81	1.93
Tease, call names	2.92	3.60	2.25	2.70	3.11	3.17	3.33	3.07
Threaten to tell	2.31	3.00	3.50	2.80	3.44	2.83	3.00	2.40

Sibling Combination*

	M1M	M1F	MM2	FM2	F1F	F1M	FF2	MF2
Asking for Help								
Ask parent for help	2.08	2.40	3.19	2.80	2.11	2.67	3.29	2.73
Complain to parent	2.08	2.20	3.19	2.80	2.89	3.17	2.67	2.80
Ask other children for help	1.62	1.40	1.00	2.20	2.22	2.67	2.19	1.73
Emotional Response								
Cry, pout, sulk	1.00	1.00	1.94	1.40	2.22	1.83	2.33	1.67
Get angry (shout, scream, yell)	2.54	3.20	3.56	2.20	3.56	3.67	3.33	2.73
Make him feel guilty	1.92	1.60	2.62	2.00	2.00	1.00	2.38	1.73
Pretend to be sick	1.62	1.60	1.63	1.80	1.56	1.33	1.48	1.47
Spook him	2.77	2.60	1.69	2.70	2.44	1.17	2.81	1.20
Miscellaneous								
Play trick	2.77	2.50	2.25	2.80	3.44	2.50	3.29	2.00
Take turns	3.08	3.40	3.19	1.50	3.33	3.67	2.95	3.07
Do something for the person	2.69	3.00	1.00	2.60	2.44	2.67	3.10	3.07
Take his things	1.62	2.00	1.88	1.90	2.00	1.00	1.86	1.27
Bother him (change TV channel)	2.77	2.60	3.50	3.30	3.11	2.83	2.81	2.60
Be stubborn, refuse to move	2.23	3.40	2.62	2.80	2.67	1.50	3.23	2.22
Give things (candy, money, toys)	3.23	1.40	2.19	2.00	2.00	2.33	2.57	2.27

*Boy with younger brother: M1M Girl with younger sister: F1F
Boy with younger sister: M1F Girl with younger brother: F1M
Boy with older brother: MM2 Girl with older sister: FF2
Boy with older sister: FM2 Girl with older brother: MF2

Table 3 *Adapted from Sutton-Smith (47)*

This Is How My Sibling Gets Me to Do What He Wants Me to Do
(95 Fifth and Sixth Grade Students) 1–5 Point Scale from "Never" to "Always"

	MIM	M1F	MM2	FM2	F1F	F1M	FF2	MF2
				Sibling Combination*				
	Violent Actions							
Beat up, belt, hit	3.00	1.80	3.06	2.50	2.44	2.33	2.67	2.22
Scratch, pinch, pull hair, bite	1.45	1.00	1.56	3.20	2.00	2.17	2.81	1.73
Tickle	2.62	2.40	2.25	3.20	3.00	3.67	3.05	2.60
Wrestle, chase	3.31	3.60	2.25	2.70	2.89	2.67	3.10	1.86
Attack things (hide toys, spoil bed)	2.38	2.20	2.31	2.50	2.67	2.00	2.38	1.80
Break things (toy, let air out of tires)	1.85	1.60	1.75	2.10	1.22	1.00	1.24	1.13
Threaten to hurt	2.92	1.80	2.13	2.70	2.44	1.67	2.33	1.80
Stop him from using phone, toys, etc.	1.62	1.80	1.19	1.90	2.33	1.50	2.71	2.08
Lock out of room	2.62	1.80	1.94	2.40	2.67	2.50	2.52	2.07
	Verbal Efforts							
Promise	3.31	3.20	3.12	2.50	3.33	2.83	3.19	2.47
Boss (say "Do it," "Shut up")	3.46	3.20	2.19	3.00	3.22	4.00	2.80	2.13
Bribe, blackmail	3.23	2.60	3.44	3.60	3.56	2.33	2.52	2.60
Ask, request	3.31	2.60	3.25	3.90	3.00	3.00	2.57	2.80
Flatter	1.62	1.00	2.00	1.20	2.33	1.67	2.48	2.00
Bargain	3.54	1.80	3.19	2.00	2.67	2.83	2.95	2.33
Tell tales	1.92	1.20	2.13	1.50	1.32	1.83	2.95	1.47
Explain, persuade	3.46	2.80	3.12	2.90	2.89	3.17	3.14	2.73
Ask for sympathy	2.31	2.40	2.44	1.70	1.56	2.00	1.81	1.93
Tease, call names	2.92	3.60	2.25	2.70	3.11	3.17	3.33	3.07
Threaten to tell	2.31	3.00	3.50	2.80	3.44	2.83	3.00	2.40

Sibling Combination*

	M1M	M1F	MM2	FM2	F1F	F1M	FF2	MF2
Asking for Help								
Ask parent for help	3.00	3.60	1.94	2.80	3.44	3.50	2.24	1.47
Complain to parent	2.46	4.50	2.13	3.20	2.33	3.50	2.81	1.27
Ask other children for help	3.23	3.00	1.94	2.00	2.44	2.83	1.86	1.53
Emotional Response								
Cry, pout, sulk	2.31	2.40	1.69	1.70	3.67	2.33	2.43	1.27
Get angry (shout, scream, yell)	3.08	3.60	2.50	3.80	3.33	3.67	3.00	2.27
Make him feel guilty	1.85	1.40	1.19	1.40	3.22	2.17	2.48	2.07
Pretend to be sick	1.62	2.00	1.44	1.50	2.11	1.67	1.52	1.47
Spook them	1.85	1.80	1.88	1.40	1.67	1.17	2.23	1.47
Miscellaneous								
Play trick	2.54	1.80	2.69	1.90	2.78	2.33	2.57	1.86
Take turns	2.85	2.80	2.56	1.60	2.11	2.33	2.48	2.13
Do something for the person	2.38	1.80	2.25	1.60	2.33	3.60	2.80	2.33
Take his things	2.15	2.20	2.31	1.50	2.22	2.50	2.24	1.86
Bother him (change TV channel)	3.08	3.60	3.50	3.10	2.67	3.50	3.10	2.80
Be stubborn, refuse to move	2.62	2.00	2.25	2.00	3.44	2.83	3.05	2.00
Give things (candy, money, toys)	2.08	3.20	1.88	2.00	2.11	2.17	2.43	2.47

*Boy with younger brother: M1M   Girl with younger sister: FlF
Boy with younger sister: M1F   Girl with younger brother: F1M
Boy with older brother: MM2   Girl with older sister: FF2
Boy with older sister: FM2   Girl with older brother: MF2

References

1. Ackerman, Paul, and Murray Kappelman. *Signals: What Your Child Is Really Telling You.* New York: Dial, 1978.
2. Ames, Louise Bates. *Is Your Child in the Wrong Grade?* Lumberville, Pa.: Modern Learning Press, 1978.
3. ———. *Child Care and Development.* Rev. ed. New York: Harper/Lippincott, 1979.
4. ——— and Joan Ames Chase. *Don't Push Your Preschooler.* Rev. ed. New York: Harper & Row, 1980.
5. ——— and Frances L. Ilg. *Your Two Year Old, Your Three Year Old, Your Four Year Old, Your Five Year Old,* and *Your Six Year Old.* New York: Delacorte, 1978–1980.
6. ——— et al. *The Gesell Institute's Child from One to Six: Evaluating the Behavior of the Preschool Child.* New York: Harper & Row, 1979.
7. ———, Frances L. Ilg, and Carol Chase Haber. *Your One Year Old.* New York: Delacorte, 1982.
8. Bloomingdale, Teresa. *I Should Have Seen It Coming When the Rabbit Died.* New York: Doubleday, 1979.
9. Brazelton, T. Berry. *On Becoming a Family: The Growth of Attachment.* New York: Delacorte/Seymour Lawrence, 1981.
10. Cain, Arthur. *Young People and Their Parents.* New York: John Day, 1971.
11. Calladine, Andrew and Carole. *Raising Siblings.* New York: Delacorte, 791979.
12. Cicirelli, Victor G. "Family Structure and Interaction: Sibling Effects on Socialization," Chapter 11 in Mae McMillan and Sergio Henao, eds., *Child Psychiatry: Treatment and Research.* New York: Brunner/Mazel, 1979.
13. Crook, William G. *Tracking down Hidden Food Allergy.* Jackson, Tenn.: Professional Books, 1978.
14. Dew, Robb Forman. *Dale Loves Sophie to Death.* New York: Farrar, Straus, & Giroux, 1981.
15. Dodson, Fitzhugh. *How to Father.* Los Angeles: Nash, 1974.
16. ———. *How to Disciplnie with Love.* New York: Rawson, 1977.
17. ———. *How to Grandparent.* New York: Harper & Row, 1981.
18. Dreikurs, Rudolf, Shirley Gould, and Raymond J. Corsini. *Family Council.* Chicago: Regnery, 1974.
19. Feingold, Ben F. *Why Your Child Is Hyperactive.* New York: Random House, 1975.

20. Forer, Lucille. *The Birth Order Factor*. New York: David McKay, 1976.
21. Gardner, Richard A. *Understanding Children*. New York: Aronson, 1973.
22. ———. *The Parents' Book about Divorce*. New York: Doubleday, 1977.
23. Gesell, Arnold, Frances L. Ilg, and Louise B. Ames. *Infant and Child in the Culture of Today*. Rev. ed. New York: Harper & Row, 1974.
24. ———. *The Child from Five to Ten*. Rev. ed. New York: Harper & Row, 1977.
25. Graubard, Paul S. *Positive Parenthood*. Indianapolis, Ind.: Bobbs-Merrill, 1977.
26. Green, Maurice R., ed. *Violence and the Family*. AAAS *Selected Symposium*. Boulder, Colo.: Westview Press, 1980.
27. Harris, Irving. *The Promised Seed: A Comparative Study of Eminent First and Second Sons*. Glencoe, Ill.: Free Press, 1964.
28. Ilg, Frances L., Louise B. Ames, and Sidney M. Baker. *Child Behavior*. Rev. ed. New York: Harper & Row, 1981.
29. Irish, Donald P. "Sibling Interaction: A Neglected Aspect of Family Life Research." *Social Forces* 42: (1964) 279-288.
30. Kohl, Herbert. *Growing with Your Children*. Boston: Little, Brown, 1979.
31. Lansky, Vicki. *Best Practical Parenting Tips*. Deephaven, Minn.: Meadowbrook Press, 1981.
32. Lerman, Saf. *Parent Awareness Training: Positive Parenting for the 1980's*. New York: A & W Publishers, 1980.
33. McDermott, John F. Jr. *Raising Cain & Abel Too: The Parents' Book of Sibling Rivalry*. New York: P.E.I. Books, 1981.
34. McIntire, Roger W. *For Love of Children*. Del Mar, Calif.: CRM Books, 1970.
35. Missildine, W. Hugh. *Your Inner Child of the Past*. New York: Simon & Schuster, 1963.
36. Moore, Raymond and Dorothy. *Home Grown Kids*. Waco, Tex.: World Books, 1981.
37. Neisser, Edith. *Brothers and Sisters*. New York: Harper & Row, 1951.
38. Rapp, Doris J. *Allergies and the Hyperactive Child*. New York: Sovereign Books/Simon & Schuster, 1979.
39. Roosevelt, Ruth, and Jeanette Lofas. *Living in Step*. New York: Stein & Day, 1976.
40. Salk, Lee. *What Every Child Would Like His Parents to Know*. New York: David McKay, 1972.
41. Sheldon, William H. *Varieties of Temperament*. New York: Harper & Row, 1944.
42. ———. *Varities of Delinquent Youth*. New York: Harper & Row, 1949.
43. Smith, Lendon H. *Improving Your Child's Behavior Chemistry*. Englewood Cliffs, N. J.: Prentice Hall, 1969.

44. Steinmetz, Suzanne K., and Murray A. Straus, eds. *Violence in the Family*. New York: Harper & Row, 1974.
45. Straus, Murray A. "A Sociological Perspective on the Causes of Family Violence," in Maurice R. Green, ed., *Violence and the Family*. AAAS *Selected Symposium*. Boulder, Colo.: Westview Press, 1980.
46. ———. Richard J. Gelles, and Suzanne K. Steinmetz. *Behind Closed Doors: Violence in the American Family*. New York: Anchor Press/Doubleday, 1980.
47. Sutton-Smith, Brian, and B. G. Rosenberg. *The Siblings*. New York: Holt, Rinehart and Winston, 1970.
48. Toman, Walter. *Family Constellation: Its Effects on Personality and Social Behavior*. New York: Springer, 1969.
49. Unknown source.
50. Visher, Emily and John. *How to Win as a Stepfamily*. New York: Dembner/Norton, 1982.
51. Wolfson, Randy Meyers and Virginia DeLuca. *Couples With Children*. New York: Dembner/Norton, 1981.
52. Zuk, Gerald H. *Family Therapy*. New York: Behavioral Publications, 1972.

Index